SERVICE WITHIN
Solving the Middle Management Leadership Crisis

Karl Albrecht

Dow Jones-Irwin
Homewood, Illinois 60430

Senior editor: James Childs
Project editor: Rita McMullen
Production manager: Irene H. Sotiroff
Jacket designer: Renee Klyczak Nordstrom
Author photo: Deborah Eck
Compositor: Eastern Graphics
Typeface: 11/13 Century Schoolbook
Printer: The Book Press, Inc.

Library of Congress Cataloging-in-Publication Data

Albrecht, Karl.
    Service within : solving the middle management leadership crisis / Karl Albrecht.
        p.   cm.
    ISBN 1-55623-353-1
    1. Middle managers.   2. Leadership.   3. Industrial management.
    I. Title.
    HD38.2.A56   1990
    658.4'3—dc20   90–33698
                                                                  CIP

Printed in the United States of America
1 2 3 4 5 6 7 8 9 0   BP   7 6 5 4 3 2 1 0

FOREWORD

Author's Note:

Göran Carstedt, CEO of Volvo Sweden, has graciously consented to contribute some ideas on internal service to this book. Volvo is widely regarded as one of the most effective companies at building and maintaining an internal culture that supports success in a competitive marketplace. Academics, writers, consultants, and practicing managers from many countries have studied Volvo management practices.

In this book Karl Albrecht once again demonstrates his deep understanding for what it takes to make service excellence happen. The unique lesson is: "If you ever hope to get things right on the outside, you first have to get things right on the inside."

His point is that there are customers in all relationships within an organization, who all need help to get their jobs done in order to make the final paying customers happy. This is no doubt a very fruitful and rewarding perspective for good leadership in the 90s.

There is no way to become a customer-oriented company without being truly people-oriented, particularly in the service industry. How can we get our workers—our colleagues—to care about the customers if they do not believe we care about them? Employees who feel they are important and who are proud of their company want to see their customers happy.

Knowing that people perform better when participating and when informed, and knowing that involvement creates better results and better quality, we have to build organizations that have a learning mode, where trust can be established. That presupposes an organization with an open dialog, close to its customers and close to its people.

Over the years, Volvo has made great efforts to build and nurture what we call the *invisible contract* with the employee. The usual visible contract tells what compensation the employee gets and what he or she has to do in return. But the invisible contract is far more meaningful; it tells what kind of a personal relationship exists between the employee and the company. It isn't written on paper, but it affects the success of the company every single day. And it has to be renewed every day by the actions of the executives and managers.

Volvo's success as a maker and marketer of cars depends heavily on its ability to perform as an organization, and we believe that ability rests on constant attention to the internal culture. In my career as an executive, I have seen many management fads and theories come and go. What has endured, and will endure, is the need for commitment on the part of corporate executives to lead rather than administrate. We must build and maintain service cultures if we are to survive and prosper in service industries. This means we have to remind ourselves on a regular basis of the important concepts Karl Albrecht explains in this book.

Göran Carstedt
Göteburg, Sweden

PREFACE

"If you're not serving the customer, your job is to serve somebody who is." "Everybody has a customer." "Quality service starts *inside* the organization."

These are the new watchwords for the service revolution. The concept of *internal service*—the idea that the whole organization must serve those who serve—has emerged as one of the most important principles of the service management approach. It is, truly, a management idea whose time has come.

Since the publication of *Service America!*, many companies around the world have adopted service management as their primary management model in their determination to achieve a competitive advantage through service quality. All of them, sooner or later, have had to face the fact that no organization can field an outstanding service product if it is at war with itself.

Probably every chief executive has, at one time or another, felt the frustration of seeing his or her subordinate division chiefs and middle managers embroiled in turf battles, feuds, and political struggles and has sensed the enormous waste of energy and talent that goes on. The thought is, "If only they would stop fighting with one another and concentrate their energies on the competitive objective, this organization could be an outstanding performer."

Many executives have become especially frustrated with "middle management inertia," i.e., the passive reaction offered by the middle management ranks to new programs or organizational initiatives aimed at cultural change. At the same time, middle managers themselves feel frustrated, demeaned, and besieged by the criticisms aimed at them. They often feel misunderstood, and many perceive themselves as scapegoats for the frustrations of both the upper and lower levels of the organization.

Now, at last, comes a new idea: *internal service* as a way to give everybody in the organization a sense of mission and purpose. The internal service concept can get middle managers out of their no-win role traps and into leadership roles where they can contribute to the success of the enterprise. And it can help people in support departments understand how to handle their functions in a way that supports the overall "service package" delivered to the paying customer.

Superior service to the customer requires the existence of a *chain of quality* that extends from the moment of truth—that all-important perceptual event in which the customer experiences the product—into and through the organization, incorporating all of the people, processes, and infrastructure that must contribute to the final outcome. The frontline contact people don't deliver the service; the *whole organization* delivers the service. They can do no better than the organization empowers them to do.

If the leaders of any service business expect to achieve and sustain an outstanding level of service quality, they must sooner or later turn their attention to the organization itself as the means for achieving their ends. The culture, the vision and direction, the leadership, the alignment of resources and functions, and the motivation and commitment of the workers are all essential ingredients for service excellence. The lesson is: if you ever hope to get things right on the outside, you first have to get things right on the inside.

The *Total Quality Service* (TQS) approach presented in this book applies equally well to service within and service without. It is a change-management process for transforming any internal support organization from an introverted, activity-focused entity to a service-driven, customer-focused one. Just as the top management team must define the strategy and direction for the company and give guidance for its attainment, so must the middle manager define a service mission and a focus for his or her part of the enterprise. This the TQS process helps to do.

Using the TQS approach, unit managers can get a clear understanding of who their customers are, what those customers need, and what the contribution of the unit has to be to successfully perform those customers' missions. With this sense of contribution clear in their minds, they can define their unit missions and proceed to educate their employees about what it takes to achieve those missions. And they can begin to make more sense out of their internal policies, procedures, and processes, making sure they are truly cost-effective and customer friendly.

One of the great realizations that emerges from applying the Total Quality Service process in organizations is that service improvement does not have to cost money. Indeed, it soon becomes obvious that it is *poor service* that costs money. Outstanding service is almost always cheaper to deliver than lousy service. Sloppy procedures, errors, inaccuracies, oversights, and poor coordination inflict enormous costs on the organization—costs which are often invisible because nobody measures them.

The cost of doing something over, as well as the cost of "damage control," i.e., recovering in the eyes of the customer, has to be figured into the actual cost of service delivery. Many of these "failure costs" go away when the organization learns, collectively, to function at a higher level of service, both within and without.

If you are a senior executive or a company owner, you need to begin educating your managers to think in terms of their internal customers, their service missions, and their contributions to the success of the enterprise. If you are a divisional or departmental manager—one of the infamous "middle managers" people are complaining about—you need to abandon the habits of activity thinking and begin to acquire the habits of customer thinking. Even if you or your people never see the paying customer, you have customers of your own. Your customers are the other people in the organization who need your help to get their jobs done. Service management is a whole new way of thinking about the job of middle management and a whole new approach to defining quality in terms of customer outcomes.

As the service revolution continues its explosive growth,

we are learning more and more about what it takes to make service quality truly a winning edge and not just a promotional slogan. I have had the good fortune, over the past several years, of observing and discovering some of the internal practices that are critical to success. The lessons are clear. Let's hope we can all learn them and put them to use.

Karl Albrecht

CONTENTS

PART II
THE PLAN FOR INTERNAL SERVICE

PART 1

THE PROBLEM AND THE OPPORTUNITY

CHAPTER 1

IF YOU'RE NOT SERVING
THE CUSTOMER . . .

There is one thing more powerful than all the armies of the world, and that is an idea whose time has come.

—*Victor Hugo*

INTERNAL SERVICE: AN IDEA WHOSE TIME HAS COME

The most often-quoted statement from the book *Service America!: Doing Business in the New Economy*, which introduced the concepts of *service management* to the United States, is:

"If you're not serving the customer, your job is to serve somebody who is."

This idea of *internal service*, more than any other presented in the book, has galvanized the attention of leaders in many industries. Executives have said, "That statement was a showstopper for me. I've always believed in the idea, but I never put it into words that simply before. When I read that, it brought the whole thing into focus."

Countless business leaders have said something like, "That's exactly what I've been trying to tell my managers for years—especially the middle managers in charge of support departments. I've always hoped they would learn to see themselves as contributors to a common cause rather than as heads of autonomous little fiefdoms that survive for their own purposes."

It's a peculiar experience having people quote you to yourself, but I have been gratified by the amount of interest in the internal service concept and by the desire expressed by so many executives to apply it in concrete ways. And I agree that, looking back from several years hence, we will probably see the internal service concept as one of the most important outcomes of the service management way of thinking. It's something the service champions seem to do better than the rest, and it's something all service businesses can use to great advantage.

Jan Carlzon, chief executive of Scandinavian Airlines System (SAS), tells his middle managers as often as possible, "You are not here to dictate to the front line, but to support and help the front line. Just because you were promoted from the front line doesn't give you the right to feel superior or more important than they are. And when they come to you with problems, you have to listen to them and help them, not the other way around."

J. W. "Bill" Marriott, second-generation head of the $5-billion Marriott Corporation, never tires of telling his managers, at every opportunity, everywhere in the world, "Take care of the employees and they'll take care of the customers." He believes leaders should support as well as direct and that there are countless opportunities for middle managers to help front-line people perform their service missions more effectively.

I've had the good fortune over the last several years of working closely with senior and middle managers in a number of service businesses in various countries to transform the service management theory into implementation, and in almost every case I've been struck by the intense interest they have shown in the possibilities of the internal service concept.

In virtually every case in which executives have sought to launch a service quality initiative, they have come face to face with the issues of organizational inertia. "How do we get the whole organization turned on to the idea of quality service?" they ask. "How do we get the back-room people turned on?" "How do we get the managers of support departments to stop feuding and bickering and work together to support the front line?"

David Luther, vice president for quality programs at Corning Glass, remarked, "We launched the most intensive program of internal culture change we had ever undertaken at Corning to recapture the market advantage we had lost to the Japanese, specifically in the area of automobile catalytic converters. We had to learn to do it better and do it cheaper, and this required a 100 percent organizational commitment.

"When it was all done, we looked back at about three years' work, and it became evident that we never really had the middle managers on board. We sort of had to drag them along with us. They never really got turned on."

This is the same kind of complaint voiced again and again by executives who have undertaken major organizational change programs. It's as if the organization presents a fundamental resistance, or inertia, to the idea of doing things in a new way. Everybody is for it, but sometimes it seems like nobody actually wants to do anything about it.

As the possibilities of the internal service approach begin to unfold, executives begin to see the basis for a complete redefinition of what life in the organization is all about. They see the possibility of working *through* the existing leadership framework, rather than *around* it. They can finally see a tool, an approach, an enabling concept that can activate their subordinate leaders and align the support resources toward the objective of service excellence.

During the several years I've been working with this internal service issue, I've seen the elements of a specific methodology evolve for getting things lined up. It has been one of those light bulbs that comes on slowly rather than in a flash, but one that throws a bright light for you once you recognize it.

It finally became obvious that the pesky "middle management problem" that is so often talked about and written about these days—the fact that middle managers are widely seen as inertial bureaucrats by those above and below them—might be solved or at least lessened by applying the internal service concept. In simple terms, let's make them into leaders who serve, not administrators who administrate.

In this work, a method eventually evolved by which middle managers can clarify their roles, redefine their contributions to the organization's success, redirect their attention and energies, refocus their resources on service to the organization, and realign their departmental systems to make it happen. This methodology has met with such enthusiastic acceptance at both senior and middle management levels that it seemed imperative to present it fully in a book.

SYNERGY, TEAMWORK, AND SERVICE EXCELLENCE

Achieving and maintaining a superior level of service that will give the company a competitive advantage starts with understanding and managing the *customer interface*. Your service only exists for the customer at the *moments of truth*, those many individual, unique encounters in which the customer experiences the business directly through his or her dealings with it. But for the moments of truth to turn out well and for all of them to add up to a quality-service image, the right things have to happen at many levels of the organization, not just at the customer interface.

It's not enough for the frontline service worker to want to give outstanding service and value for the customer's money. He or she can't do it alone. There has to be a *chain of quality* that extends beyond the worker, to the support people in the back room, to the supervisors and managers who guide the operation, to the many support departments that have to make things happen at the right places and right times, and to the senior managers and executives who look after the whole business.

All of this must work together like an orchestra performance. The orchestra is the company, the chief executive is the conductor, and the business plan is the score. Yet it seems that most service businesses, especially large ones, operate more like undisciplined rock and roll bands. The right things may or may not happen at the front line, but as you progress backward into the organization, disorder and disarray are more in evidence than they should be. "Customer focus" is often a catchphrase at best, and at worst it is never mentioned. "Turf" becomes sacrosanct.

Boundary disputes drain precious managerial energy.

Rules take precedence over reason, and the sanctity of internal procedures outweighs the appeal of creative approaches to bringing the customer back.

Hardly anybody would argue against the concept of internal service, i.e., the idea that all of the people, structures, and resources in the organization should be aligned behind the moments of truth to create the best possible impact on the customer's perception of service quality. But in most companies it goes no further than lack of argument. It is typically a case of benign neglect. Everybody believes in serving the customer, but apparently most of them want to get out of it.

It's a curious fact in most service businesses that the lowest-quality people in the work force are the ones placed in contact with the customer. Contact people are usually the newest, youngest, least experienced, least knowledgeable, least trained, and lowest paid. And yet they are the ones who are in charge of the all-important moments of truth. Their supervisors may also have to deal with customers from time to time, but they usually have "more important" things to do. In addition, there is a whole cast of support people who don't deal directly with the customer, and most of them like it that way. It becomes clear to every newcomer who starts at the bottom of the totem pole that the customer interface is the bottom. In most service organizations, things are set up to encourage people to want to "graduate" *away* from the customer interface.

This interesting state of affairs creates two competitive handicaps: (1) we put the lowest-quality resources at the all-important customer interface and (2) we allow those not involved in the interface to scatter their energies and have their behavior driven by all manner of internally generated demands on their time. It's almost as if the quality of the customer interface and the degree of support for that interface are left to chance. And yet, everything we know about competitiveness in a service market tells us it should be the other way around.

Let's explore this phenomenon a bit further; it invites a deeper understanding. Probably the main reason people gravitate away from customer contact jobs is that they are generally "harder" jobs, psychologically speaking. There is an element of "emotional labor" involved in constantly interacting with strangers throughout the day. They are all different, they come at you in a never-ending stream, and they all want something from you.

Working with invoices or computer printouts in the back room is different; you have some control over how you spend your time. You can exercise some choice in your activities; you can do things in your own time and at your own pace. But on the front line, the customer calls the tune. He or she shows up wanting service, and you have to respond then and there. And there is the ever-present element of satisfaction; the customer decides, at that moment, how good a job you have done. Even if it is a silent judgment, you know it has been made. This is emotional labor, and most people find it taxing.

Being a manager is even more fun than being a back room person. You get to structure your day in your own way, at least to a large extent. You can move around more freely, talk to people, hang out with your cronies, and have some solitude when you need it. Somebody else takes care of the never-ending stream of wanting customers. Somebody else reacts to their demands, handles their complaints, calms down the angry ones, explains the unexplainable policies to them, apologizes to the ones who have been wronged, and tries to get them to come back and buy again.

So there is a natural human tendency to prefer work that is somewhat more autonomous and not paced by the arrival events in the customer stream. Of course, some people thrive on personal contact work, but they are all too few. Some enjoy the steady, frequent interaction with new people, the challenge of meeting their needs, and the satisfaction of sending most of them on their way happy. But if you ask most people what kind of work they really prefer for their careers, not many will answer you in terms of frontline contact jobs, especially since those jobs are not usually highly paid.

This natural tendency to gravitate away from the customer creates the second handicap mentioned above, i.e., the tendency of "internal" people to forget about the realities of the customer interface and to define their daily activities in the language of a completely separate realm of endeavor. "We're the computer department," or "We handle purchasing," or "This is the finance department," are all expressions of self-definition that largely exclude the paying customer from the collective consciousness.

It's a real challenge for internal people in a service organization to think, act, and talk in terms of the relationship of whatever they do to the success of the business in the customer's eyes. But this is what happens in the best service companies. You can never have everybody 100 percent on board all the time, but in the outstanding service organizations, the majority of internal people have learned to see what they do in the context of the company's success in its market.

What we must seek in the management and operation of service-excellent businesses is nothing less than complete *internal synergy*. This is the focus of energies made possible by a shared concept of what the business is all about, the alignment of resources behind the delivery of the service product at the moments of truth, and the teamwork made possible by each group's understanding its contribution to the success of the enterprise.

This book is an attempt to formulate a methodology for achieving this synergy by applying the internal service concept.

A BRIEF RECAP OF SERVICE MANAGEMENT

It is necessary to set up a conceptual foundation for explaining how to apply the internal service concept. Arising as it does from the framework of *service management*, which I have explained in *Service America!* and *At America's Service*, it takes its cues from certain transformational ideas which you must understand clearly in order to put it to use.[1]

For that reason, a brief recap of the key ideas of service management is necessary here. For the sake of those who have read those two aforementioned books, this will be mercifully short and perhaps a useful reminder. For those who are completely unfamiliar with the service management model, I strongly recommend you read or browse at least one of those two books before reading this one to help set a foundation for the thinking process presented here.

It is critical that you understand that service management is a very specific management model with certain key ideas and implications not found in the contemporary manufacturing model of management we all learned in our business careers. It is much more than just a fluffy idea about being nice to the customer. It has several important and potentially radical things to say about how to structure work, how to lead people engaged in service missions, and how to communicate to people about quality in a service environment.

Service management is a total organizational approach that makes quality of service, as perceived by the customer, the number one driving force for the operation of the business.

Please reflect on the implications of this definition. Although brief, it has several critical components which invite careful understanding. First, it is a *total organizational approach*. It affects everyone in the organization, from the chief executive to the lowest ranking person at the front line. It is an overriding philosophy, a way of doing business, a way of managing, and a way of rewarding.

Second, it focuses on *quality of service* as the hallmark of success. Service management rests on the conviction that, if you have properly conceived of service quality in market-success terms, you can meet your business and financial objectives by concentrating your attention, energies, and resources on achieving that quality standard. In other words, if quality is there, profit will be there as well.

Third, service management recognizes no other standard for quality than the quality of service *as perceived by the customer*. It doesn't really matter what you think the service is worth. The customer has the last vote, and he votes with his money. This means that it is crucially important that you understand what the customer considers service quality to be, how he or she values it, and how—at all times—the service you provide stacks up against those critical criteria.

And fourth, service management recognizes the quality of

service as perceived by the customer as *the number one driving force for the operation of the business.* This means that quality of service should have an influence, either direct or indirect, on everyone's job. There must be a constant assessment and reassessment of each job, each department, each system, each policy, each procedure, and each management action in terms of its contribution to the success of the business in the eyes of the customers.

Another important characteristic of service management as a way of thinking is its focus on the *customer interface* as the starting point for all management action. Whereas the conventional "Harvard Business School" model of manufacturing-oriented management starts with *structure* and *process*, service management starts with *outcomes.* This alone is a profound realignment of management thought, and it deserves some careful consideration. A later chapter will develop this point in greater detail.

Scandinavian Airlines' Jan Carlzon frequently makes a statement which causes debates, questions, and havoc with the thinking of many executives. He says it simply, unequivocally, and without qualification: "The only thing that counts in the new SAS is a satisfied customer."

It comes down to a means-versus-ends orientation. Bob Nugent, chief executive officer of Foodmaker, Inc., operator of over 1,000 Jack-in-the-Box hamburger restaurants says, "We've committed ourselves to making a hit with the customer. Our research tells us we have the right service-quality model for the customer interface, and I'm quite comfortable with the idea of letting the bottom line show how well we do it.

"You know," he said, "it occurs to me that trying to run a business by keeping your eye on the bottom line is kind of like trying to hit a home run by keeping your eye on the scoreboard. It doesn't work. You've got to keep your eye on the ball. Hit the ball right and the scoreboard has got to show it."

That may be the most important piece of advice any executive can give another. Of course it's important to have good financial management, which includes good cost control, but accountants don't run businesses; they merely report on them. They ride on the back of the boat and tell you where you've been. It's an essential contribution, but let's remember where it fits.

Moments of Truth

Another critical difference that's part of the service management model is a new focus on the nature of the product and, at the very same time, a new focus on the way workers work. This is the basis of the concept of *moments of truth.*

> **A moment of truth is any episode in which the customer comes into contact with any aspect of the organization and gets an impression of the quality of its service.**

The term originated in Spanish bullfighting as *el momento de verdad,* or the final moment at which matador and bull face each other alone. It is a critical episode, and it must come to a resolution. Jan Carlzon of SAS popularized the term with statements like, "We have 50,000 moments of truth every day." Actually, it was first adapted by Richard Normann, a Swedish management consultant who played a key role in the formulation of Carlzon's market strategy.

Of course, we'd like to use the term without its confrontational overtones, to suggest that customer and service providers come into contact at many critical episodes, and the customers form their impressions of service quality at these many contact events. Collectively, they all add up to the total service image of the business.

We can take this figure of speech—moment of truth—and make it a very literal, concrete part of an approach to producing, delivering, and managing service. By moving the focus of attention from job descriptions and tasks to moments of truth, we can help the service worker think more clearly about his or her contribution to customer satisfaction. We can also help the manager think more clearly about service quality: it is excellence at the moments of truth, excellence as defined by the customer's frame of reference.

The service management philosophy suggests that everybody has a part to play in making sure things turn out right for the customer. Certainly anyone who is in direct contact with the customer should feel responsible to see things from the customer's point of view and to do whatever is possible to take care of the need. But everyone else needs to have the customer in the back of his or her mind also. Under the service management philosophy, the whole organization should operate like one big customer service department.

The service management approach seeks to build a service culture that makes superior service to the customer a recognized mission for everyone in the organization, including the managers. It begins with the responsibility of top management to define the business mission and to specify the strategy needed to make service quality the key to the operation of the business. Once managers at all levels are ready to understand, support, and contribute to the service mission, they will begin doing the right things to help the frontline people take care of the customers. Instead of flogging the employees for poor service, managers must provide the leadership and support they need to help them do an outstanding job.

If you take the moments-of-truth concept literally and concretely, you forget about jobs and tasks and organizational structures and procedures, and you start thinking in terms of outcomes. You can immediately begin to take an inventory of the moments of truth your customers experience as your frontline people deliver the service. Once you know what these moments of truth are, you can analyze each and every one of them from the standpoint of quality. You can start improving the ones that need improving and looking for ways to add value to all of them.

Note that a moment of truth is typically neither positive nor negative in and of itself. It is the outcome of the moment of truth that counts. Did the customer feel good about the price of the airline ticket? Did he or she find the right seat, or was the seat double-booked? Was the flight attendant friendly or surly? Did the flight leave on time, or was it delayed? If it was delayed, how caringly did the gate agent or pilot explain the delay to the passengers?

Keep in mind that not all moments of truth involve direct interaction between your employees and the customers. There may be other moments of truth besides those. When the customer sees an advertisement for your business, that's a moment of truth; it creates an impression of some sort. Driving by your facility is, for the customer, a moment of truth. Entering a parking lot, walking into a lobby and getting an impression of the place, receiving a bill or a statement in the mail, listening to a recorded voice on the telephone, getting a package home and opening it—all of these are events that lead to an impression of your service. The sum total of all of the possible moments of truth your customers experience, both human and nonhuman, becomes your service image.

As you think about this new view of your product in terms of moments of truth as episodes that offer perishable opportunities to make a quality impression, it begins to become obvious that management is not in control of the quality. Managers can't be present at all of the moments of truth to supervise them and make sure the employees handle them properly. This means that they have no choice but to rely on the working people who are handling the moments of truth. In fact, they are the managers at those moments; they are managing the moments of truth.

This is a provocative concept; every service employee is a manager, in a way. Each one controls the outcome of the moment of truth by having control over his or her own behavior toward the customer. If the service person is apathetic, disagreeable, unfriendly, cold, distant, or uncooperative, his or her moments of truth go to hell in a handbasket. If he or she is lively, pleasant, warm, friendly, cooperative, and resourceful in taking care of the customer's problem, then his or her moments of truth shine, and the customer tends to generalize those experiences to your overall service image. It may be a frightening prospect for some managers: the ant-army is in charge.

Critical Moments of Truth

Not all moments of truth are created equal. In a typical high-contact service business, there may be over a hundred different kinds of moments of truth, but usually a few of them will have a critical impact on the customers' perceptions.

These critical moments of truth warrant special care and feeding. Managers can't be everywhere at once, so they need to choose carefully those aspects of the operation that have the highest potential impact—positive or negative—on the customer's satisfaction and repurchase intention. They need to keep surveillance over these special aspects of the product and help the service people handle them effectively.

CYCLES OF SERVICE

The next step in the service management reasoning process is the realization that moments of truth do not stand alone; they come in bunches or clusters. A customer doesn't call up and say, "I'd like to buy a moment of truth, please." What happens is that the customer decides to do business with your organization and goes through a *sequence* of moments of truth, all of which add up to a total service experience or *cycle of service.*

A cycle of service is the continuous chain of events the customer goes through as he or she experiences your service. This is the natural, unconscious pattern that exists in the customer's mind, and it may have nothing in common with your "technical" approach to setting up the business. You may be conditioned to think of your service operation in terms of the organizational departments and specialties that have to get involved in order to deliver the service.

But the customer seldom thinks in terms of departments or specialties. He or she usually thinks only in terms of having a need and having to take action to get that need taken care of. The customer thinks in terms of an objective: I want a place to store my money; I want to eat a good meal in pleasant surroundings; I want to have my teeth cleaned; I want to see more clearly; I want to get to Buffalo in time for the wedding; I want to get my car working properly again.

It is quite common for service businesses to give their customers the runaround because of the way they are organized. The customer turns the car over to the service-order writer, hoping to have it repaired. Returning to pick it up, he finds he must go to the cashier to pick up the keys and pay the bill.

There is no one for him to talk to about the car—no one to answer his questions about the peculiar sound in the engine. If he doesn't like the bill or disagrees with the charge, the cashier may say, "I'm only the cashier. You'll have to see the service manager." When the customer asks, "Where is the service manager?" the answer might be, "He's gone for the day. You'll have to come back tomorrow." The customer may ask to speak to the mechanic who worked on the car, only to be told that the mechanics aren't allowed to leave the shop to talk to customers.

Transfer this example to any other service industry or setting you like—banks, hotels, hospitals, financial services, food service, transportation—virtually all of the well-established business sectors, and you can find variations on the same situation. It seems difficult for the organization to react to the customer in terms of his or her need rather than in terms of its internal structure, especially if the customer has an unusual or complicated problem or a nonroutine need for which the business doesn't have a "system." More repeat business has probably been driven away because people could not gain access to

FIGURE 1–1
The Cycle of Service

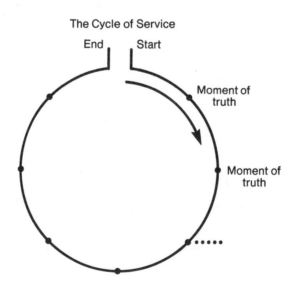

The Cycle of Service

someone who could take care of their problem or alleviate their concerns than for any other reason.

The cycle-of-service concept helps people help the customer by getting them to reorganize their mental pictures of what goes on.

Figure 1–1 illustrates the cycle of service graphically.

The basic building block of service is no longer the employee's job task; it is now the moment of truth he or she *manages*. The employee no longer manufactures the product; the employee is *part of* the product. Quality is no longer satisfactory performance of assigned duty; it is now defined as the *outcome* of the moment of truth.

Just like the moment-of-truth concept, the cycle of service is a powerful idea for helping service people shift their points of view and see things as the customers see them. Analyzing and improving cycles of service is a basic part of the "engineering" process of service management.

THE SERVICE TRIANGLE

One of the most basic elements of the service management model is presented in *Service America!*, and one which many managers use in discussions, is the *service triangle*. It is worth repeating here for continuity, and it will play an important part in our analysis of the success factors involved in implementing a service initiative in just about any kind of organization.

Virtually all of the excellent service businesses we know about have three critical characteristics in good measure. These three key success factors become the three corners of the service triangle.

They are:

1. A vision, or strategy, for the service product.
2. Customer-oriented frontline people.
3. Customer-friendly systems.

The service triangle is a way of diagraming the interplay of these three critical elements that must perform together to

FIGURE 1–2
The Service Triangle

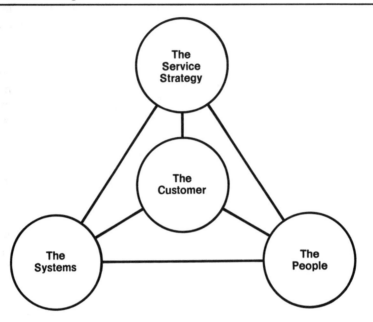

maintain a high level of service quality. The following explanation comes verbatim from *Service America!*.

> *A well-conceived strategy for service.* The outstanding organizations have discovered, invented, or evolved a unifying idea about what they do. This service concept, or service strategy as we shall call it in later discussions, directs the attention of the people in the organization toward the real priorities of the customer. This guiding concept finds its way into all that people do. It becomes a rallying cry, a kind of gospel, and the nucleus of the message to be transmitted to the customer.
>
> *Customer-oriented frontline people.* By some means the managers of such organizations have encouraged and helped the people who deliver the service to keep their attention fastened on the needs of the customer. The effective frontline person is able to maintain an "other-worldly" focus of attention by tuning

in to the customer's current situation, frame of mind, and need. This leads to a level of responsiveness, attentiveness, and willingness to help that marks the service as superior in the customer's mind and makes him or her want to tell others about it and come back for more.

Customer-friendly systems. The delivery system that backs up the service people is truly designed for the convenience of the customer rather than the convenience of the organization. The physical facilities, policies, procedures, methods, and communication processes all say to the customer, "This apparatus is here to meet your needs."

These three factors—a clear service strategy, customer-oriented frontline people, and customer-friendly systems—are all relatively simple in concept and fairly easy to understand. Yet making them a reality is almost always a monumental task, especially in large organizations. Most of the remainder of this book *(Service America!)* deals with what we have found out about implementing service management by trying to actively manage these three critical factors.

Service management is a transformational concept. It is not a collection of platitudes, buzzwords, or clichés about how "the customer is always right." It is a unified approach to running a service business that focuses on the moments of truth that make up the total customer interface. Success in a service business is no longer a matter of managing the organization, but of managing the *customer's experience with* the organization.

Ultimately, all of the precepts of service management come together around the idea of a *service culture*, which is an organizational climate, environment, or work context—call it whatever you like—that values quality service as a business priority and impels everyone in the organization toward that end. A service culture is, at one and the same time, the means for achieving an outstanding level of service and the evidence of its attainment.

With this brief synopsis as background, let us proceed to put together the pieces of the internal service puzzle and see how the internal service concept can form the basis for a whole new approach to organizational synergy, teamwork, and middle management leadership.

CHAPTER NOTES

1. Portions of the text in this chapter are taken from or adapted from both *Service America!* and *At America's Service.* This is to preserve continuity among the several books on service management and to be sure the concepts are explained in a relatively uniform way.

CHAPTER 2

NEW MANAGEMENT THINKING FOR THE SERVICE AGE

Man's mind, stretched to a new idea, never goes back to its original dimension.

— *Oliver Wendell Holmes*

As the service revolution unfolds, it is having an ever broader impact on the ways organizations do business. In particular, it is forcing us to re-examine some of our basic ideas about marketing, competitive differentiation based on quality, and organizational management practices. Executives, management thinkers, and management writers are advancing new ideas and new points of view for the consideration of service and the management of service.

Some of these emerging new precepts deserve special attention here because they can help to clarify the issues that arise in moving toward a customer-driven, service-oriented culture. Developing a strong internal culture of service depends to a great extent on having clear and workable ideas about the organization's relation to its customer as well as its internal climate and operating mechanisms.

Here I would like to review several of the more compelling of these new precepts—some of which are really old ideas given new life—and show how they will influence management thinking in the decades to come. Some of these ideas I have briefly mentioned in *At America's Service*. I would like to pull them together here for continuity and to show how they interrelate. In some cases, I have drawn excerpts from *At America's Service* for certain areas of the following discussion. It seemed more appropriate to use that same material in these few cases rather than to rephrase it merely for the sake of saying it differently.

THE PASSING OF THE
MANUFACTURING MODEL

Management thinking in most parts of the industrialized world is currently trapped in a kind of time warp. Executives and managers of hundreds of thousands of large and small companies in service industries are still trying to run their businesses with old-style manufacturing thinking, manufacturing theories, and manufacturing methods. We are long overdue for an enlargement of the frame of reference we use to run businesses, whether they are manufacturing businesses or service businesses.

Actually, we need to abandon the arbitrary distinction between "service" businesses and "manufacturing" businesses altogether. With the advent of the service management model, the distinction is now grotesquely obsolete. There really is no such thing as a company that is not in the service business. Everybody has to think about service, defined as the sum total of all value delivered to the customer, whether tangible or intangible.

The only real distinction anymore is the relative proportion of tangible and intangible value sold and delivered. In the coal business, the emphasis is on the tangible. But if the intangibles of the customer interface go unmanaged, the coal will eventually stop moving as well. Conversely, the banking business deals with a highly intangible product, i.e., the handling and movement of information, but if the tangible aspects of the customer's experience go unmanaged, the customer revokes the bank's privilege of handling his or her data.

So the service revolution brings us to the brink of a new age, one in which the focus of success is more clearly recognized as the *total customer interface*. We will need to abandon arbitrary distinctions such as "product" and "service" and begin describing things in terms of *perceptual events*, i.e., moments of truth, which influence the customer's attitude about the value we provide for his or her money. These moments of truth involve tangibles and intangibles, and each one takes its place in the total mosaic or customer approval.

What does it mean to say that we are still trying to use manufacturing approaches to run service businesses? Is this just a cute figure of speech, or does it have concrete implications? How do we recognize the effects of this phenomenon, and what shall we do about them?

The answers to those questions are not simple. They don't exist in the form of quick one-liners. They emerge as a result of careful consideration of the problems facing service businesses today. They are realizations one comes to after reconsidering these issues in the context of the service management model and facing some of the contradictions that arise.

In my previous book, *At America's Service,* I devoted a chapter to the argument that the "General Motors" model of management and its financially oriented conceptualization preached by the Harvard Business School and virtually all of the famous American "ivy league" universities is dying. Chapter 6 of that book, titled "General Motors Management Doesn't Work for Service," talks about the failure of the GM/Harvard approach to solve the problems of internal culture, employee attitudes, and service quality. For a full discussion of that argument, please consult *At America's Service.*[1]

In using the terms *General Motors management* and *Harvard management,* I do not mean to disparage either of those two venerable institutions. I merely want to use those names as an easily recognizable shorthand for the standard management approaches that are so widely accepted internationally in corporate management. Most likely, the major business schools in the United States and other countries are experiencing an evolution of thought as they see the service revolution unfold. But I have the distinct impression that few of them are really at the forefront of this thinking as of yet.

For the sake of this discussion, I will try to encapsulate several key elements of the discussion from *At America's Service.* The following statements are strong generalizations and not intended to apply in all cases or for all time. But they do represent, I believe, a fair comparison between "GM thinking" and "service management thinking."

Means versus Ends. While the GM/Harvard precept of management seems to be to watch financial performance carefully and maximize profitability by conservative use of physical and financial capital, the service management precept is to watch customer preference carefully and maximize profitability by winning and keeping customers. It's not so much that one is wrong and the other is right, but that there is a shift in emphasis. Service thinking argues that if the quality of service is there the profit will follow.

Process versus Outcome. While GM/Harvard thinking concentrates on predefined normative measures of employee behavior, i.e., job-task performance, service thinking concentrates on outcomes measurable at the customer interface, i.e., the moments of truth. GM/Harvard methods work well for jobs involving standardized outputs you can measure and count, but they fall apart quickly when it comes to knowledge-based jobs or those involving unpredictable customer events. Service thinking emphasizes *less* definition and control, not more. It invites the employee to become a strategist and manager of his or her particular moments of truth. This approach contradicts the underlying precept of GM/Harvard management that tends to try to define all jobs in normative terms.

Structure versus Culture. The Harvard/GM approach conceives of the company as an *organization*, i.e., a structured set of abstract elements. The service management approach conceives of the company as an *organism*, i.e., a collection of people who form a culture. One focuses on things, the other on people. GM/Harvard thinking approaches the executive task in terms of defining the rules for how the boxes on the organization chart should operate and interrelate. Service thinking views the executive task as one of leading through culture, not administrating through systems.

As executives in more and more organizations feel the frustration that results from trying to legislate good service, i.e., tighten up the job standards and "manage" the people into treating the customers well, it begins to dawn on them that "you can't get there from here." Or, in the words of philosopher Aldous Huxley, "There's no right way to do the wrong thing." They come to believe that it's the culture and the systems that need fixing, not the people. They realize they face the challenge of making service quality a belief system and a way of life for the organization, not a set of rules to be enforced.

With the passing of the manufacturing model and the striving toward a cultural model for service excellence comes a whole new set of realizations and new ideas about service products, service workers, service work, and the management of those.

The entire frame of reference of western management is seriously in need of updating. This process is already happening in the boardrooms, meeting rooms, and work places of the top service firms around the world. It will be interesting and educational to watch it unfold.

NEW ECONOMIC THINKING: MANAGING THE INVISIBLE ASSETS

With the passing of the manufacturing model and the movement toward service thinking in businesses, there seems to be a growing feeling among many senior executives that the traditional precepts and points of view of financial management may be misguided as well. There is a sense that, not only do the balance sheet and income statement not tell the whole story of the organization's status and possibilities, but the story they do tell may be misleading—not misleading in the sense that the actual numbers don't say what the accountants claim they say, but misleading in the sense that there is an untold story just as important as the one being told.

The untold story, which never seems to show up on the financial statements, is the story of the *invisible assets*. These are the elements of the organization's existence that play a crucial role in its success and failure, but which conventional accounting practices ignore completely.

I first got impressed with this way of thinking in response to a remark made by SAS' Jan Carlzon during an interview in the training video program "Service Management."[2] Carlzon commented:

> Look at our balance sheet. On the asset side you can still see so-and-so many aircraft worth so-and-so many billions. But it's wrong. We are fooling ourselves. What we should put on the asset side is "last year SAS carried so-and-so many happy passengers." That's the only asset we've got: people who are happy with our service and are prepared to come back and fly with us again. We can have however many aircraft we want, but if they don't want to fly with us, it's worth nothing.

This, I believe, is a profound statement that reflects a profound realization. It is a conceptual "switcheroo," a change in the angle of attack on the whole question of assets and their deployment for profit. Before we dismiss the statement as just a clever piece of rhetoric, let's examine the germ of the idea behind it.

Carlzon is saying, in effect, that we ought to recognize, measure, think about, and manage an asset that the accountants don't even carry on the books: *the loyal customer base.* Marketing theorists estimate that it costs up to five times as much to win a new customer as it does to make a repeat sale to an existing customer. This suggests that the cost-of-sales component will be less for a large loyal customer base than for a small one. In effect, the loyal customer base spins off revenue—and, presumably, profit—almost on its own, whereas the "disloyal" customer population must be wooed and won at higher cost.

Nowhere on the typical balance sheet is there an asset category called "loyal customers who will buy from us in the future." Accepted accounting practices forbid it, and the laws and policies of financial disclosure would consider it a form of financial chicanery to try to do so. Yet, the loyal customer base clearly is an asset of some kind, isn't it? And investing in it can enhance profits, can it not?

This example crystallizes what a growing number of economists are calling a crisis in corporate financial thinking. They are beginning to argue that the entire assumptive basis of management accounting as we know it today is fatally flawed. It tends to steer managers, they believe, toward a pattern of resource utilization that may not be wise and which certainly does not help them chart the most successul long-term course for their businesses.

According to H. Thomas Johnson and Robert S. Kaplan in their landmark book *Relevance Lost: the Decline and Fall of Management Accounting*,[3] most of the accounting practices of today evolved to meet the demands of people outside the corporation for information. Investors, governments, regulators, and financial analysts all want "hard" information: monetary measures of assets that can be traded on the market. Even though the real selling price of a business is usually higher than the book value of its assets to the extent of its "invisible equity" such as the value of patents, image and reputation, experience of its work force, skill of its management, and the like, the balance sheet shows only tangible assets that can be produced in an audit.

There is nothing intrinsically wrong with this type of asset measurement. It works for certain purposes. What is desperately wrong is that boards of directors, senior executives, and managers all down the line usually mistake the balance sheet for the reality of the business. They believe what it says because they've been brainwashed by the "bottom-line" theology. For generations, the bottom line has served as a convenient intellectual bludgeon in the hands of those who think and operate conservatively. Whenever someone wants to appear practical and savvy about business or wants to kill some new proposition he doesn't like, he will usually start throwing around terms like "bottom-line impact" and "return on investment." These terms seem to be strangely absent, however, when the same person favors moving ahead with some exciting project of his own.

Other economists have commented on another destructive element of accounting practice, especially as used in American businesses. This is the habit of reporting sales and earnings on a quarterly basis, which has the effect of making boards of directors and chief executives nearly paranoid about short-term performance. Some have even argued that part of the competitive edge Japanese firms have gained over their American counterparts comes from their habit of reporting financial results on an annual basis rather than quarterly.

For an American firm to incur a huge expense to improve its operations with a view toward a profit impact a year or two later is to court disfavor with the financial community because of the short-term impact. Japanese executives, on the other hand, can think and operate on a longer-term basis and tend to feel more comfortable about resource investments that have longer-term payoffs. This "quarterly roller-coaster" syndrome is so characteristic of American business that it may cause many management teams to opt for the safe course in the short term at the expense of greater financial success in the long term.

Some executives become so slavishly beholden to the short-term bottom line that they lose all courage and willingness to risk on behalf of their companies. They spend too much of their time buried in financial reports and analyses, most of which say one thing: "Don't." They unconsciously conceive of their roles as based on conservation of assets rather than building real value.

Actually, I believe there are at least five categories of invisible assets executives should be paying attention to:

1. The loyal customer base.
2. The image and appeal of the company's product line.
3. The loyal, committed work force.
4. The service culture within the organization.
5. The strength of its management.

Each of these deserves an in-depth consideration, but space does not permit that here. However, I would like to take just one of these items and argue the value of an asset management philosophy on its behalf. This is for the purpose of building a case for thinking about the invisible assets in concrete terms.

Let's consider the loyal, committed work force as an example of a neglected invisible asset that can have a huge impact on the organization's success. Consider two competing companies, Company A and Company B. Company A invests a significant portion of its funds over the years in recruiting, hiring, placing, training, developing, nurturing, motivating, and advancing its people. Its executives see training and development as absolutely essential to putting a quality service product on the market and positioning itself in the customer's mind as a good place to do business.

Company B invests next to nothing in its work force. Its executives see training and development as an "extra," a line-item budget category that gets a little bit of money in the fat years and gets cut first in the lean years. They see turnover and employee disgruntlement as facts of life and assume they will always have a relatively green, minimally skilled work force.

Question: Other factors perceived as equal, which company would you expect to fare better in its market place, Company A or Company B? Presumably, Company A should do better, if they have done a good job of developing their people. And it probably does. Now comes a significant question: If the executives of Company B want to achieve a superior level of service and gain a better market position, can they justify investing in their people if they invoke contemporary accounting principles?

Under currently accepted accounting practices, money spent to train, develop, and motivate the people in the work force gets posted to the general ledger as an *expense*. When the invoices come in to pay for the training consultants or cover the costs of training equipment, materials, and facilities, the accounts-payable clerk posts them as reductions to cash and increases to account categories such as "training expense." If you know a little bit about double-entry bookkeeping, you realize that this outflow of money has the effect of *decreasing* the net worth of the business: i.e., it reduces shareholder's equity.

But the company is clearly better off as a result of having workers who are more qualified, loyal, motivated, and committed. Yet there is no way to show it on the balance sheet. In fact, it looks like the company is worse off, financially speaking, than it was before it made the investment. Company B's accountants would be hard-pressed to recommend spending heavily on employee development, especially if the company already happens to be in red numbers.

What should happen, but which cannot happen under current financial theory, is that the money spent on developing the people should show up as an *asset transfer*, not a cost. We have actually transformed a cash asset into another type of asset, namely competitive ability derived from a better work force.

Precisely the same line of reasoning applies, I believe, to the other four categories of invisible assets mentioned previously. Because we can't measure them, we can't value them. If we can't value them, we find it hard to muster the courage to invest in them, especially if it looks like we're reducing the balance-sheet value of the business.

Certainly, just about every executive has reflected on the benefits of protecting and enhancing these invisible assets from time to time. These are not new issues in the sense of the need to do something about them. What is new is the realization that neglecting these assets is a consequence of the long-trusted "bottom-line" approach based on double-entry accounting practices that originated back in the middle ages. We are coming to understand that executives have more important things to do than look at balance sheets and income statements.

Robert Riley, group managing director of the Mandarin Oriental Hotel Group for Asia, commented recently on the need to keep means and ends clearly identified. He says, "I spend as little time as possible looking at the financials. They're very important, but I have a first-rate comptroller who goes over them and discusses them with me. Then I can spend as much of my time as possible helping these hotel managers and their people deliver an outstanding product that will bring in the business and make the financials come out right."

Foodmaker's Robert Nugent agrees. "Ours is a 'top-line' business," he says. "Our cost structure is very characteristic of the fast-food industry. The more food we sell, the more profit we make. What we have to spend our time on is attracting customers to generate the sales. We can't do that by sitting around staring at P&L's. We do it by working with our restaurant managers to figure out more ways to help them sell hamburgers and related products. Certainly the financial figures are extremely important, but we think the action is in putting superior products on the market and merchandising them well."

LIFETIME VALUE OF A SINGLE CUSTOMER

Another key concept that is fast taking hold in service management thinking is the idea of keeping the customer for life. This is not by any means a new idea, but rather one that executives are now according a much greater degree of respect. For many years, Harvard's Ted Levitt has contended, "The real objective of any business is to get—and keep—customers."

This neat phraseology stops being a platitude when you examine the day-to-day workings of a typical service business and see how many customers they regularly abuse, with no real effort to build appreciation, loyalty, or repurchase intention. Sure, people mouth slogans like "The customer is king," "Customers count with us," and "The customer is always right." But when the customer wants a refund, has a special problem of some sort, asks for something out of the ordinary, or can't decide what he or she really wants, watch what happens.

If the organization can't "process" the customer with one of its standard mechanisms, the tendency is to try to get rid of the customer. An angry customer gets treated to a rebuttal more often than listened to. A customer who is disappointed with the quality of what he or she purchased gets "pacified" more often than satisfied. And when something goes really wrong, the typical business tends to react by letting the customer rant and rave and then hoping he or she will just go away. The art of the simple apology is rare in business. And the art of skillful recovery and restitution to capture future customer loyalty is even more rare.

One of the most useful and enlightening activities you can include in your company's service management training program is to ask people, individually and collectively, to estimate the lifetime sales value of a typical customer. Not all customers will stay in your service population for life, and not all of them will live long, but it's very interesting to arrive at a hypothetical figure for what one customer could spend with your business over, say, 20 or 30 years. In this activity, I often ask each person in the room to write that amount on a stick-on nametag and put it on the front of his or her clothes. Then, during the discussion of how to get and keep customers, this figure comes up again and again as a way to focus attention on the value of superior service.

For a product such as an automobile, for instance, a person might well spend as much as two to three times his or her annual salary over a lifetime. With the prospect of this kind of long-term revenue, does it make sense to get into a shouting match with the customer over a small charge on the repair bill? When the old-timers of the retail business tell you, "You never win an argument with a customer," they mean that you might keep the money but lose the customer. Time, money, and effort spent in retaining a customer, even at the expense of short-term profit, is usually well spent.

Progressive bank executives are beginning to think in terms of a life-cycle model of the financial services customer. As a person grows from infancy through adolescence, teenage years, young adulthood, middle adulthood, middle age, and senior years, he or she is a candidate for different kinds of financial services at each stage. Most banks, unfortunately, seem to operate on the unconscious principle of *extracting value* rather than *giving value*. That is, they seem to look upon the customer as an opportunistic source of revenue to be extracted at every turn by devices such as "service charges," bad-check charges, late payment fees, and all manner of nicks and gouges that the customer sees as punitive and exploitive rather than as adding value to his or her life.

When a bank realistically embraces the idea of lifetime value, it has to think about *value delivered*, not *value extracted*. Executives find that this concept of serving and marketing to the same individual, unique customer at all key financial occasions along his or her demographic lifeline virtually forces them to rethink their policies and procedures. It also causes them to rethink approaches to selling new business and extending business with current customers. And it even starts to affect the design of their data processing systems, making them more sales oriented and service oriented, and not so much product oriented as they typically have been.

The "LCV," or *lifetime customer value*, concept has implications far beyond simply treating the customer pleasantly. It begins to affect the basic operations of the organization, and—in great measure—its culture.

MANAGEMENT'S ADDED VALUE

What do managers really contribute to the quality of the product the customer buys? In what ways do they add value to the process of originating and delivering the tangibles and intangibles that make the organization successful? The concept of *cumulative added value* has become fairly popular in organizational analysis, especially in manufacturing sectors. This is the idea that as the product—either tangible or intangible—progresses from nothing to its final form as the customer first experiences it, each employee involved with it adds value in some way. Each person's contribution adds equity in a way that presumably increases the value and, indeed, the price the company would ask for the product.

Question: If employees are supposed to add value to the product, should we also think of management as adding value to it? How can we justify charging the customer enough for the product to cover the cost of the chief executive's salary, accommodations, and benefits, as well as those of all the other executives and managers who don't deal directly with the customer or product? What, indeed, is management's added value?

One of Peter Drucker's most insightful comments, in my view, was, "Much of what we call management consists of making it difficult for people to get their work done." When I think back about the management jobs I've held, ranging from military officer to R&D program manager, to new-product development manager, and as an owner of several small businesses, I realize that much of what I considered "management" involved doing things that served my own needs to feel "in charge." Some of the ideas I'd learned about direction, visibility, and control were really part of what I have now come to call the "neurosis of management."

The traditional approach to management impels managers to "know what's going on." They must "be on top of things."

They must not "let things get out of hand." A truism that virtually every new manager hears sooner or later is "Surprise is the enemy of management." Yet it is arguable in many cases whether the rules, controls, and reporting processes imposed on working people by managers really contribute to organizational performance. Might it be that they just make managers feel powerful and secure? And might they actually be wasting the workers' time and energy, which might go to more productive use?

There is a near-paranoid fear on the part of many managers about not knowing what is going on and about allowing workers too much freedom. One of the powerful appeals of the standard model of management seems to be that it plays to the appetite that exists in so many managers for control and certainty. *Things* are easier to measure and manage than people, and the task-structure-process approach makes managers feel good.

Yet it is becoming more and more clear that the manufacturing model brings with it certain side effects that are very difficult to fix. In service environments, it typically leads to overdirection, overcontrol, and constant demands for status reporting. These management neuroses, and the kind of work climate they tend to create, can stand in the way of mobilizing the best efforts of frontline workers who are operating at the moments of truth. There seems to be a mind-set that favors system solutions over people solutions.

What about the possibility that many managers may be extracting value rather than adding value to the process? Could it be that unnecessary policies, rules, directives, instructions, meetings, and demands for information set up by managers have the effect of *reducing* the available work energy for producing and delivering the product? Might it be that, in looking for cost-saving opportunities in the organization, we should start by reducing the costs imposed by the management process rather than reducing the employee labor cost?

This *value-added management* concept will take shape more clearly and become more compelling as time goes on, I believe. Here are some of the elements of potential added value we might consider for managers:

1. *Focus*—helping everyone in the organization target their energies on the success priorities of the business.
2. *Alignment*—helping the various units orient their plans and activities toward the overall mission.
3. *Culture*—establishing, teaching, preaching, and reinforcing the primary values and the philosophy needed to achieve the organization's mission.
4. *Collaboration*—removing the obstacles to a shared-fate feeling of cooperation and teamwork; helping to replace fences with bridges.
5. *Development*—investing the organization's resources carefully for the development of the invisible assets that lead to its success, especially the development of its people.

MANAGEMENT AS A SERVICE

Following on from the idea of added-value management, we must recognize that in a service culture the practice of management becomes in itself a service. Without giving up their responsibilities for setting direction, allocating resources, establishing priorities, making decisions, and guiding the work, managers must broaden their concepts of their roles to include supporting and enabling the frontline workers in their handling of the moments of truth.

Part of the transformation in thinking that happens as executives and managers work to move their organizations toward a service management style of operation is a rethinking of issues relating to managerial control, employee discretion, and the flow of energy. By "flow of energy," I mean the sense of action and influence that gets the work done. In the old manufacturing culture, managers tended to see themselves as pushing, pulling, and steering the workers into getting the work done. In the service environment, they tend to see themselves as enabling rather than controlling.

The idea of management as a service comes naturally to many managers, although they might not have phrased it in that particular way. For others, it may offer a new and interesting clarification of their roles as leaders. And, for others, it might seem like so much baloney. Some traditionally schooled managers will have trouble with "all this touchy-feely crap," as one manager I know calls it. Sadly, many other managers see this "soft-side" view of leadership as an intellectual aberration, although they have no alternative to offer in the face of the classical problems of employee alienation, demotivation, and disaffection. You, as a manager, must make your own determination about the idea of management as a service and how you can best work with your people to achieve high-quality service.

If you find the idea of management as a service appealing and potentially practical, here are some things you can do to begin applying it in a concrete way:

1. Regularly ask each of the people you supervise, "What can I do to help you do your job better?" "What problems do you have that I can help you solve?" "What's getting in the way of your doing the best job you possibly can?"

2. Think of things on your own that might contribute to their effectiveness. Identify innovations—improvements in your computer systems, streamlining of procedures, or changing relationships among jobs or units to help them collaborate better.

3. Have regular meetings with the people in your group to review the effectiveness of the whole operation; ask them to identify any organizational procedures, processes, or systems they feel need rethinking or elimination; make cooperation and mutual effectiveness a regular matter of discussion and analysis.

4. Stop wasting their time with directives and demands that have no other purpose but to feed your management neuroses; review every single policy, procedure, rule, or regulation you have ever established from the point of view of its contribution to the effectiveness of the people doing the work; eliminate every report you can possibly do without; overcome your anxieties about being "in charge," and let them get back to work; you'll know when they need you.

THE CONCEPT OF EMOTIONAL LABOR

Another important concept which affects the management of service businesses is the recognition that working directly and interpersonally with customers involves a form of "emotional labor." Emotional labor is any kind of work in which the employee's *feelings* are in some ways the tools of his or her trade. That is, the person's psychological, emotional, creature reactions get involved as a consequence of some aspect of the job itself. Feelings are in some way a part of job performance.

Examples of jobs that involve extreme degrees of emotional labor include psychiatrist, social worker, doctor, nurse, paramedic, firefighter, and police officer. These people have to deal directly with other human beings on a regular basis and often with people who are in various states of distress. It is very difficult to do these kinds of work without having the feelings of the afflicted people rub off on the person doing the work. After all, the patient in therapy only has to deal with one distraught, maladjusted person—him- or herself—while the psychiatrist has to deal with a number of them during any working day.

Service jobs and, in particular, public-contact jobs can involve a relatively high degree of emotional labor. A person who handles lost-baggage claims all day for an airline, for example, deals with a lot of disturbed people. Not too many of them are happy, and seldom does a traveler stop by the lost-luggage counter to wish the person behind it a pleasant day.

Psychologists have identified a distinctive reaction in human beings called the *contact-overload syndrome*. It befalls people whose job situations put them in one-to-one contact with many, many people on a constant, repeated basis. Think about a person who processes driver's license applications all day long or rings up meals for hundreds of people at the cashier position in a busy cafeteria or processes hundreds of telephone stock transactions each day. Having to interact with one stranger after another, over and over, all day long, causes a kind of emotional fatigue reaction to set in. A person can handle just so many of these miniature emotional events in a given period of time before he or she begins to feel tense, overloaded, tired, and jaded. How many times have you heard a service worker say, "I just can't bear to look at another customer today"?

It appears that some people can tolerate high-frequency contact much more than others. Some people just find it too uncomfortable and psychically draining to deal with a steady flow of strangers for hours on end. In other words, people vary in their ability to handle emotional labor. This is a fact that many managers have not fully appreciated; in fact, most of our management theory has overlooked it entirely. But emotional labor affects both the worker and the customer in very direct ways.

When employees are stressed, psychologically overloaded, fatigued, or disgruntled, it shows up in their interactions with customers. As Paul Goodstadt, director of service quality for National Westminster Bank, puts it, "Unhappy employees are terrorists. Whether they mean to or not, they destroy service quality right at the grass roots."

NEW LEADERSHIP PRACTICES FOR THE SERVICE AGE

One of the most important new realizations that we are coming to in the management of service businesses is that service workers need good leadership, even more so than is the case in other kinds of work. If we are going to ask the person in contact with the customer to operate more self-reliantly, to use greater imagination and initiative in solving customer problems, to be more skillful in handling the interpersonal processes, and to think on his or her feet at the moments of truth, we're going to have to provide that person with a different kind of supervision than we have offered in the past.

For one thing, service people are going to need less "management" and more leadership. In other words, bosses are going to have to learn to run things less by administrative rules and procedures and more by circumstantial guidance and support to the employees who must handle many different kinds of situations. Leadership training will almost certainly be an important element of service management training in the future.

More and more organizations are making a major commitment to leadership training as an essential element of their service quality programs. The Natural Gas Company in Sydney, Australia, uses the four-quadrant leadership model developed by the highly respected Australian consultant Wilf Jarvis in all of its management training. Says CEO Len Bleasel, "We believe high-quality leadership is one of the most important things we as a company owe the employee. We insist that every single manager go through the four-quadrant leadership training and put its concepts and methods to use."

Similarly, Scandinavian Airlines has set up what it calls the SAS Leadership College to develop and implement leadership training for all of its managers. Says John Mott, head of the college in Copenhagen, "We recognized that we needed to place a much greater emphasis on the leadership role of all of our managers. People in this business tend to manage by rules and regulations more than by personal influence. We want to make sure all SAS managers have the basic training and indoctrination that will help them not only to manage, but to lead in a service environment."

People involved in emotional-labor jobs, as just explained, also need a special kind of care and feeding, and this affects the roles and behaviors of their leaders. They need encouragement, understanding, support, and appreciation. They also need relief from time to time. Frontline supervisors must be tuned in all the more closely to the psychological well-being of these people, because they are affecting the quality of the customer interface on a daily basis.

Another critical element of the new service leadership approach is a much higher awareness of the element of *discretion* on the part of the service worker. Whenever the frontline employee has to turn to his or her supervisor for a decision, say about a refund or a special request, it not only slows the customer down, but it also conveys an impression of lack of trust. It tends to make the customer feel the company doesn't trust him or her and also that the company doesn't trust the employee to do the right thing.

We must begin to train service leaders to recognize opportunities to enhance service quality by putting the frontline people more completely in charge of the moments of truth. We must also train and orient the employees better, make them better informed about business decisions, and give them better support for their roles as ambassadors for the company as well as service workers. Then we will be in a position to entrust them with a much greater degree of autonomy and decision making. We can truly make them authorized to think.

In reviewing a great deal of literature dealing with leadership and leadership training, I've concluded that we need to make the concept of leadership much less esoteric and psychological if we want to get a large number of frontline supervisors to embrace it. Most of the leadership training I'm aware of seems to emphasize elements of interpersonal psychology, influence, and group dynamics, which many frontline people find somewhat cerebral and sometimes threatening. They sometimes come away from leadership training with the idea that there is some undefinable "something," such as personal charisma, which they are supposed to have. Many times, they don't know where to start when they go back to their jobs.

What is needed, I think, is a model for service leadership which brings the service interaction into clearer focus and which tells frontline supervisors in very simple terms how to approach various elements of the employee's assigned functions in terms of relative degrees of discretion to be granted and relative levels of support needed from the leader. There is not sufficient room for a thorough treatment of the topic here, but the amount of space devoted to it is in no way indicative of its importance. It is a critical issue, and I hope to have more to offer about it in the future.

INTERNAL MARKETING: YOUR EMPLOYEES ARE YOUR FIRST "CUSTOMERS"

Another important precept that is rapidly gaining recognition in service management cultures is the idea of *internal marketing*. If your employees are not sold on the quality of the service your organization provides and on the importance of their roles in providing it, there is no way on earth they will ever be inclined to sell your customers on it. You must think of the employees as a "market," in a sense. By this I mean you will literally have to sell the idea of service quality to them. In many cases it will be an easy sell; in some cases it will be a very difficult one. You need to make sure they believe in the idea of putting the customer first and that they take seriously the organization's efforts to do so.

For a major service program to succeed in your organization, a necessary first step will be to win the commitment of the people who ultimately control its success: the frontline working people. Commitment requires that they:

1. Understand the objective and the need for achieving it.
2. Believe in the program and feel it is worthwhile.
3. Believe that it has the possibility of succeeding.
4. Feel that it will be personally worthwhile for them.

These criteria pretty well suggest what you have to do to win their commitment.

First, you must be able to conceptualize the program's objective clearly and simply. You must have a compelling reason to undertake it and a compelling explanation of that reason. You must be able to dramatize the value of the effort in human terms. And you must be able to explain it to everyone, every day, in simple and compelling language.

Second, you must be able to show clearly how the program will appeal to the customer and consequently how it will benefit the organization. You need more than platitudes at this point. You need demonstrable evidence of the impact service quality has on the customer's choices about where he or she does business or about how he or she is willing to spend money. You need to have your homework together for your own sense of conviction as well as to support the convictions of the frontline people.

You need to have a program plan and an overall philosophy of implementation that can make sense to the rank-and-file working people. You need to have credibility with them so that when you publicize your program and your plan they will be willing to embrace it as making sense. Your plan has to show evidence of unwavering top management support and the willingness to invest the necessary resources to make it work. If you go to them with nothing but a batch of platitudes, slogans, and pep talks while the plan shows that you really don't intend to make an investment in service quality, they will smoke you out. They know when top management is serious and when it's not.

And finally, the whole undertaking must proceed in the spirit of cooperation, support to the frontline people, and teamwork all across the organization. The objective must carry with it the possibility that the mission of achieving it will be personally rewarding in some way. It does not necessarily have to be a promise of more money, although that is usually one of the most appealing payoffs. But people have to genuinely feel that the program is being undertaken with their support and commitment, not by trying to drive them into it. There needs to be some element of pride in the company and a sense of meaning in taking on the challenge.

You will probably have a bigger selling job with your managers than you will with your employees, particularly with the middle managers. The frontline supervisors typically respond to the same kinds of appeals as the workers because they share many of the same experiences and views as a result of their tactical orientation to the work itself. Typically, however, the middle managers have trouble figuring out how to participate energetically in top-down programs of the type required to launch a major service-quality commitment.

What often happens is that top management gives the go-ahead to a big new service venture on the assumption that the middle managers understand it, believe in it, and are as excited about it as the chiefs are. In reality, they may just be smiling and "shining you on," giving the impression that they are "on board." Thereafter, they may do little or nothing to drive the program forward. They probably will not do anything consciously to impede the program in any way, but neither will they lend their energy, enthusiasm, or creativity to it. They may become what middle managers are often perceived to be: an inertial blob of Jello in the middle of the organization, neither helping nor hurting, but just sitting on the bench.

Middle management inertia is by no means universal, of

course. In some organizations the middle managers tend to grab the ball and exert very strong leadership in support of what they believe in. In other organizations there may be general inertia at the middle levels, but there may still be individual managers who are highly proactive and visionary in their leadership. But in general, given the historical image of middle managers as inertial bureaucrats, it makes sense to test very carefully to see what kind of commitment is there, which managers really have it, and what kinds of personal skills they have for making a service program successful.

This early process of commitment building can be crucially important. Without energy and commitment, the organization itself will become its own worst enemy. With it, most of the obstacles and pitfalls will eventually give way to the energy and drive that lie behind the commitment.

"TQM": THE LAST GASP OF THE MANUFACTURING MODEL[4]

With the passing of the manufacturing model and the advent of service management comes the need for new approaches to the issue of quality. One would have to be living in a cave these days not to have heard at least something about the "quality movement" in business today, especially in the United States but also in many other western industrial countries. There seems to be a feeling in American business circles of concern and downright indignation about the fact that many Japanese companies have outstripped their American competitors in product quality, largely as a result of an almost fanatical application of quality management methods in their factories.

This competitive backlash has triggered a search for ways to mobilize whole companies toward the goal of quality—doing whatever they do outstandingly well for the purpose of competing more effectively. This is especially true now in companies in "service" industries.

As the search progresses for management methods that can bring about the hoped-for quality revolution, two major alternative approaches present themselves for consideration. One is much more well known. The other, although less well known so far, will, I believe, eventually emerge as the methodology of choice for achieving superior service quality. In the following discussion I will review both avenues and disclose my biases about which offers the greatest long-term promise.

Basically, executives of service organizations are being presented with two quite different conceptual alternatives for embarking on a service quality campaign. One is the standards-based approach, which is a holdover from manufacturing quality control methods, and the other is the culture-based approach, which is newly emerging from the application of service management. At this point, you can probably predict which approach this book will advocate.

Standards-Based Approaches

The standards-based type of approach to service quality is the use of predefined *service standards* as management tools. This approach typically involves the analysis of service jobs, formulation of objectively measurable standards of performance, and management action to ensure that the employees meet the service standards. This is a characteristically authoritarian approach that has certain advantages but suffers from certain drawbacks as well.

Setting standards for service quality and then managing in order to meet them works well in some industries and some types of businesses, particularly those in which it is relatively easy to measure job performance in objective terms. Many organizations use service standards as the focus of their initial efforts at improving service quality. The two best known standards-based approaches currently in use are the American Total Quality Assurance (TQA) approach, recently renamed "TQM," or Total Quality Management, and the Japanese *kaizen* approach. Both have their origin in manufacturing industries, which affects their applicability in service organizations.

The Total Quality Management, or TQM approach, is based largely on the work of W. Edwards Deming, an American consultant whose work had a profound influence on Japanese manufacturing management. Other consultants, notably J.M. Jourand and Philip Crosby, have adapted these methods to American industries. Indeed, the current American interest in Japanese manufacturing methods and management approaches is a kind of reverse importation of technology, largely stimulated by the phenomenal success of Japanese manufacturers in penetrating U.S. markets with products offering higher quality and lower cost than U.S. products.

The best-known U.S. exponent of the TQM process is Philip Crosby, widely recognized as the father of the "Zero Defects" philosophy and developer of a 14-point quality improvement process. Crosby, more than any other practitioner, has made the TQM process available to a large number of managers in many organizations.

The essence of the TQM process is the idea that *quality work is that work that meets a predefined standard.* If you have no standard, you have no way of measuring quality and consequently no way of managing it. So TQM is all about defining standards, identifying the obstacles to achieving those standards, and working to remove the obstacles. The ideal organization is that in which everyone knows what his or her quality job standards are and achieves them. The focus of management in this context is to see to it that the workers have what they need in terms of tools, methods, materials, and skills to meet their quality standards.

A variation of the TQM process is a Japanese method based on the so-called *kaizen* concept. The Japanese word *kaizen* refers to a philosophy and a process of incremental improvement in quality of work through the combined efforts of many employees, each making his or her individual contribution to the big picture. To the Japanese way of thinking, many small improvements on the part of many workers are just as valuable as a single major improvement brought about by management analysis.

The kaizen process, promoted largely by the Cambridge Institute in Tokyo under the direction of Masaaki Imai, is a worthy competitor to the Deming/Crosby approach in the United States. In the kaizen method, employees work together in groups to identify and correct shortfalls from quality standards.

They draw upon the services of process experts within the organization to help them develop solutions to quality problems. Typically, when they eliminate the causes of a shortfall in quality, they are able to achieve a higher level of quality than the standard dictates, and consequently management resets the standard to a higher level. The kaizen process is a management-led approach that attempts to engage the contribution of all employees in production-type jobs.

The exponents of the approach are attempting to apply it to white-collar activities as well, but with somewhat less satisfying results.

The advantage of standards-based approaches such as TQM and kaizen is in the simplicity and teachability of their methodology. Each provides a clean, logical framework for implementing quality improvement processes throughout an organization or at least in those areas where objective standards are possible.

The disadvantage of all of these approaches is that they were born in a manufacturing era, and they have a predominantly manufacturing mind-set at their foundation. Because a service product is profoundly different from a manufactured product, users of these methods find it difficult to take into account the psychological and cultural factors that may be crucial to service quality.

The current attempts by TQM advocates to apply the process to service organizations is, in my view, a misapplication of a technique which is well proven in manufacturing organizations but which does not fit well with service organizations. At the risk of seeming overly critical, I have come to consider the rush to TQM—for service businesses—as the last gasp of the manufacturing model before it dies and is superseded by a whole new conceptualization based on service management principles.

I believe TQM has worked very well in the domain to which it applies, and there is a great need to continue to exploit its benefits in organizations whose primary activity is manufacturing and dealing with highly tangible processes. I believe some of its tools and techniques can be subsumed into a new, broader concept of quality management based on cultural approaches.

The Need for Culture-Based Approaches

Culture-based approaches are those that focus on the social context of the workplace with the hope of establishing an ethic of commitment and enthusiasm for service quality that will lead to autonomous efforts on the part of workers to improve and maintain the quality of service on their own, especially in areas for which the service process is so varied that it does not lend itself easily to rational performance standards.

That is, they accept ownership of the values behind service excellence, and they take responsibility for customer "superfaction" as their personal missions without necessarily having to have managers set and enforce standards for them.

The need for a culture-based approach to service quality becomes more and more clear and compelling as you study the ways in which the outstanding service organizations operate. Virtually all of them operate more by culture than by coercion, more by motivation than by mandate, more by shared values than by standards. This is not to say that objective standards do not play an important role—quite the contrary. But the standards are tools for excellence rather than ends in themselves.

In the search for a service quality methodology, I have concluded that cosmetic approaches are clearly not cost effective and that standards-based approaches are more suited to manufacturing organizations than to service organizations. I believe that *culture-based* approaches will ultimately emerge as more effective for the management of service.

A culture-based approach is, in some ways, more difficult to conceive and implement than a standards-based approach because every organization has a different culture and therefore a different starting point for the development of a service quality ethic. "Culture" is a much less concrete concept than the concept of job standards. It is more difficult to define, more difficult to analyze, and more difficult to change. Yet the possibilities for competitive success through the development of a service culture are inviting and exciting. The approach may be somewhat more "artistic" than analytical, but there are many well-proven methods of analysis and design that we can bring to bear.

"TQS™": THE NEW MANIFESTO FOR CHANGE MANAGEMENT

After a number of years of involvement in the implementation of service quality programs and having the opportunity to discuss the matter with executives of outstanding service organizations, I have concluded that what is needed is not a standard "formula" for a service program, but rather a *methodology system* for transforming the organization, not a fixed recipe or a "one size fits all" process, but a logical system of methods and tools that can be brought to bear in a unique way for the special needs of a particular service organization. I have evolved a process called *Total Quality Service*, or *TQS™*, which is a change management process for helping the organization become what it needs to be to achieve superiority in service.

TQS™ is a set of five interrelated methodologies for assessing, defining, and improving service quality. Each of the methods has something special to offer at a certain point and under certain circumstances. By selecting the appropriate mix and sequence of these methods, we can develop a service quality program that has the maximum chance to succeed in a particular organizational climate.

The five key "methodology menus" involved in the TQS™ process are:

1. Market and customer research (MCR).
2. Assessment, measurement, and feedback (AMF).
3. Strategy formulation (SF).
4. Education, training, and communication (ETC).
5. Process improvement (PI).

Figure 2–1 shows how these methodology choices fit together in the TQS™ concept. The following discussion describes each methodology area in more depth. As you read them, please bear in mind that the sequence in which these methods are applied will depend on the situation that exists in the organization, the market and competitive situation, and the leadership style and attitudes of senior management.

FIGURE 2–1
The TQS™ Model for Total Quality Service

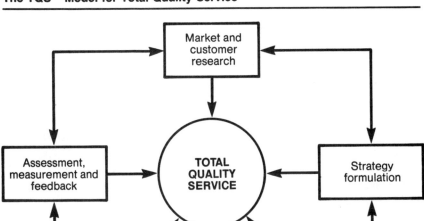

© 1988 Karl Albrecht.

Market and Customer Research (MCR)

There are two main kinds of research needed in the TQS™ process: market research and customer perception research. Market research, in the context of this discussion of service quality, is the investigation of the structure and dynamics of the marketplace the organization proposes to serve. This includes segmentation analysis, demographics, niche analysis, product/customer match analysis, and analysis of competitive forces.

Customer perception research goes at least one step deeper than conventional market research. It attempts to understand the thoughts and feelings of the customer toward the service product and the service provider in hopes of discerning one or more critical factors in the customer's perception of the product. This type of *psychographic* research can give invaluable information about how the customer sees the service product as presented and what he or she is really trying to buy.

Strategy Formulation (SF)

At times it may be necessary for the organization's executives to review various aspects of the competitive strategy or possibly even to rethink the mission, strategy, and basic direction. In such a case, the methods of Strategy Formulation come into play. Indeed, it may be difficult for the executives to do the things necessary to build service quality until they have a clear definition of what the service product is, to whom it will be sold and delivered, and what level of quality will be required to compete effectively.

Education, Training, and Communication (ETC)

The methods of education, training, and communication come into play in helping everyone in the organization understand the service philosophy, service strategy, service product, and service quality standards. Some of these methods are organizationwide, serving to build awareness and commitment. Others are more targeted to specific aspects of service quality. And others are aimed at helping employees acquire specific skills and knowledge they need to handle service jobs well.

Process Improvement (PI)

A key part of any wall-to-wall service quality program is a means for grass roots efforts to improve the various processes, systems, methods, tools, policies, and procedures involved in the delivery of service. These process improvements can originate with management analysis of the organization or from the initiative of frontline people who want to improve the work processes they are involved with.

Note that the process improvement sector of the TQS™ model subsumes the kinds of activities that traditionally go on in the TQM process. In addition, it includes a variety of simple pencil-and-paper tools that frontline employees can easily learn and use to attack service quality opportunities on their own.

Assessment, Measurement, and Feedback (AMF)

Sometimes a simple "service audit" is the thing that will get the ball rolling and get people to think about service quality. By evaluating the service levels in various areas of the organization and getting managers to think about the results, it may be possible to focus people's thinking on the customer interface and the need to improve it.

In other situations, management may feel the need for a much more thorough assessment of the service quality. It may be appropriate to develop a measurement framework and gather reliable data with which to evaluate the service product. This is certainly an essential process in the long run. Assessment, measurement, and feedback may be an appropriate place to start in some situations, but not necessarily in all.

Applying the TQS™ Process

As you can see from Figure 2–1 and the various methodology menus given above, the five major components of the TQS™ process work together to build service quality. There is no one starting point for all programs or all organizations. Where you start depends on where you are.

For example, in an organization that has a strong habit of measurement and analysis, it may be most comfortable to start right out with service audits, standards development, and the installation of a service quality measurement system (SQMS).

This could allow the executives and managers to proceed from a basis they understand and feel comfortable with. The next steps in their program would flow from the data made available by this "AMF" component of the process.

On the other hand, if the organization has done very little measurement and analysis of its activities in the past and if its leaders tend to "ride to the sound of the guns," they might feel more comfortable starting with market and customer research as a way to get a clearer fix on the organization's image and positioning. They may want to deal with matters of mission and strategy before trying to measure service quality or set standards.

In yet another situation, the executives may feel that

awareness and commitment are crucial—possibly because of a routinized "manufacturing" type of culture which lacks a customer focus. They may choose from the methods of the "ETC" methodology menu, i.e., education, training, and communication, to start managers and employees thinking about service and service quality. They may decide to use training programs, companywide communication events, or internal video programs to call attention to the focus on service and to begin enlisting the support of the organization for a major initiative.

In the three vastly different examples just cited, there are ways to begin that can be highly successful and ways to begin that can lead to disappointment. The appropriate starting point for the process, the appropriate sequence of activities, and the appropriate choice of methods all depend heavily on the organization's current state and the orientation of the executives who lead it. This is probably one reason why so many service programs fizzle or run aground: the choice of methodologies is often not appropriate to the situation.

This is a key aspect of the TQS™ process: its flexibility and adaptability for many different types of organizations in different situations. Whereas most of the standards-based approaches previously described are based on a fixed recipe of steps, regardless of the history and current status of the organization, the TQS™ process explicitly recognizes the need to customize the methodology to the individual organization's own reality. This requires a good deal more skill and judgment on the part of those involved in designing the service quality program, but it is more likely to yield a program strategy and an implementation plan than can achieve the goal of service excellence.

I believe the TQS™ model is more valid for service businesses and approaches the issues of quality service and quality management from a necessarily broader perspective. It enables us to link everything we do to the customer interface and to be sure that all quality development efforts have the potential of paying off in the market place.

CHAPTER NOTES

1. Karl Albrecht, *At America's Service* (Homewood, Ill.: Dow Jones–Irwin, 1988), p. 82.

2. *Service Management*, video published by Coronet/MTI, distributed by Shamrock Press, Division of Karl Albrecht & Associates, 1277 Garnet Avenue, San Diego, CA 92109. (619) 272-3880. See also "Service Within," also featuring Karl Albrecht, from same source.
3. H. Thomas Johnson and Robert S. Kaplan, *Relevance Lost: The Decline and Fall of Management Accounting* (Boston: Harvard Business School Press, 1987).
4. Portions of this section are excerpted and adapted from an executive discussion paper, "Total Quality Service™: The Methodology for Service Excellence" (San Diego: Karl Albrecht & Associates, 1988). © 1988, Karl Albrecht, all rights reserved. Used here with permission.

CHAPTER 3

THE ORGANIZATION: ENEMY OF SERVICE

> We trained hard—but it seemed that every time we were beginning to form up into teams, we would be reorganized. I was to learn later in life that we tend to meet any new situation by reorganization, and a wonderful method it can be for creating the illusion of progress while producing confusion, inefficiency, and demoralization.
>
> *—Petronius Arbiter*

When it comes to internal service and the prospect for synergy—or the lack of it—many organizations seem to be their own worst enemies. The rules, procedures, and departmental lines of responsibility often have the effect of conspiring to prevent the various groups from working together as a team. Too often, structural craziness, irrational systems, nonsensical policies, turf wars and boundary disputes, and sheer interdepartmental friction and competitiveness are the enemies of service rather than the helpers.

Too many organizations are at war with themselves as a result of the way they have organized and deployed resources and the way they have divided up responsibilities. If the leaders of any organization ever hope to deliver an outstanding level of service to the external, paying customer, they must devote their attention to cleaning up the act inside. The backroom processes must make sense if the customer is going to experience an outstanding service product. Let's look at the primary ways in which the organizational structure can work against service excellence.

THE PRODUCTION MENTALITY

There seems to be an automatic tendency in organizations to depersonalize the discussion of business. We almost always seem to gravitate toward topics and terminology based on *things* rather than on people. This may be an artifact of the male value systems that dominate most organizations, or it may simply be that most people are more comfortable dealing with things than with human beings. So we turn the people into things in our minds, and then we can think about them more comfortably.

Because we need to count and measure in order to manage, we tend to spend a lot of time thinking about revenues and expenses, passenger-miles, hamburgers sold, surgeries performed, "covers" sold in the restaurant, policies issued, or whatever it is that happens. But we don't automatically tend to talk in terms of the *people* who flew in the airplanes, ate the hamburgers, gave up their gall bladders, visited the restaurant, or took out the insurance policies. We are a thing-oriented business culture, not a people-oriented one.

This is not entirely a bad situation, but it does have certain profound effects on the attention, perception, and thinking processes of the people who work inside the organization and of those who manage it. They automatically tend to think in terms of internal structure and process rather than in terms of interactions with customers. This leads to a state of affairs in which structure is the dominant motif in management thinking, and, in the absence of a customer focus, it leads to decisions about how to structure and organize that may not be the best for the customer.

There is a powerful unconscious tendency in most organizations to evolve structures that serve the internal convenience of those who work with them, rather than the convenience of the customers affected by them. This is one reason, perhaps, why so many airport terminals seem to be designed for the convenience of maintenance crews in moving airplanes and equipment around, not for the convenience of customers in getting from the parking lot to their assigned seats.

Banks tend to epitomize this internal-convenience design

focus. Banking hours have traditionally been set up for the convenience of the bank employees, not for the customers. Many people can't get to the bank during normal working hours, and most banks are closed by the time they get off from work. Hospitals also tend to have very inconvenient and "unfriendly" customer-impact systems. Many people describe the treatment they get in health-care facilities as "being processed like cattle," or "being treated like a thing." The systems are there for the people doing the work, not for those being worked on.

This holds true for internal service organizations just as much as for customer contact departments, sometimes even more so. There is a tendency for a support department to build or evolve systems and ways of operating that make it easy for it to minimize its own work load, keep track of data, reduce variations in procedure that can lead to errors, and reduce the need for follow-up with the "customer."

In order to make these systems work, the department has to bamboozle its customers into doing things its way. The result is often that the internal customers or departments have to put up with less than what they consider an adequate response, live with peculiar or inconvenient procedures and paperwork processes, waste time and energy waiting for bureaucratic procedures, and sometimes have to do part of the job themselves.

Organizations, more often than not, are the enemies of service. Nobody wants it to turn out that way, but without a very strong determination to make systems consistently customer-friendly, they usually turn out to be organization-friendly at most and sometimes not even that.

An internal service department becomes a production-bound bureaucracy when it:

- Tries to force its customers to follow inconvenient procedures.
- Tries to impose unnecessary paperwork burdens on its customers.
- Refuses to make people available for advice and assistance.
- Rejects the legitimate requests of its customers for help.
- Tries to push part of its own work load off onto its customers.

- Cuts back on service levels in favor of its own internal resource needs.

It makes sense for the leaders of any internal service department to conduct an honest audit of its service activities to find out whether it has become production-bound and bureaucratized. If it has, they have an obligation to the rest of the organization to reorient the priorities.

SYSTEMS, POLICIES, AND PROCEDURES

Neil Hodges, head of the service quality task force in the State Bank of South Australia in Adelaide, learned an amazing lesson when he began analyzing organizational systems and procedures in the bank:

> I asked for an audit of all our forms. I was curious to know just how we looked to the customer in terms of our paper and procedures and what we looked like internally. I was amazed to find that we had over 1,500 forms in use in the bank and that we were creating 100 new ones a year.
>
> That just blew me away. How in heaven's name can you think up that many different forms? There's no way we can be using all of that rigmarole effectively. I immediately made it one of my priorities to chop out as much of that paper jungle as possible.

Neil Hodges' approach reflects a growing tendency among service-oriented executives, a tendency to get much more aggressive about the creeping bureaucracy that exists in all organizations. They are becoming aware of and alarmed by the fact that the administrative underbrush is strangling the operation, hindering rather than helping employees in doing their jobs, and making the organization look like a ponderous bureaucracy that's imprisoned by its own red tape.

Organizations these days are much more information-intensive than ever in the past, and a consequence of having to move a lot of information around is that you have to have methods for doing it. There arises an almost "invisible factory" for information. People manufacture, store, transport, warehouse, and consume information much as they do physical products. This goes on so long that it takes on a separate reality all its own. People begin to think, not in terms of the underlying thing they want to accomplish, but in terms of the information media they have to manipulate to get it done.

Instead of "getting other opinions on this plan," it becomes "send it around for staffing." Instead of "estimate the resources your department will need," it becomes "send in your budget." Instead of "let us know what item of equipment you need to purchase," it becomes "prepare and submit a purchase request."

People have become info-bureaucrats. There is a confusion of means and ends, and it is so profound and all-encompassing that most people don't realize it. They go right along, pushing papers as if the movement of the paper were an end in itself.

This introverted preoccupation with paper and procedure often engenders a certain myopia about the objectives of the information in the first place. Take, as a simple case in point, a typical bank statement. Presumably the bank statement is supposed to be a communication from the bank to the customer. This means it should tell the customer the kinds of things he wants to know in a form that makes it easy for him to understand and interpret it. But many bank statements are so cryptic, poorly organized, and uninformative that the customers have trouble understanding them.

Out of curiosity, I recently looked at the format and layout of the statement from the bank that my firm uses for its main accounts. One of our staff was having great difficulty reconciling the statement to our computerized accounting system. She found a number of cryptic items on the statement labeled "Bank Originated Entry." The statement provided no explanation about any of these items. She observed that one of the "bank originated" additions was for exactly twice the amount of a bank originated deduction. She finally figured out that the first entry was a bank keying error, which entered a deposit as a deduction. The bank employee reversed the error with a second entry in the form of a deposit for twice the amount of the error. Nowhere on the statement did the bank explain what it had done. The bank's internal systems and procedures made sense to the people working there but made no sense to the customer trying to reconcile the statement. This customer-unfriendly system was causing so much extra work for our staff members that my business manager finally called a meeting with the bank manager and explained the problem to him. That led to a change in bank procedures, which resulted in more information accompanying the statement.

Another good example of an internal information system, which very few people consider, is the simple paycheck. In many organizations the computer spits out the paychecks, and each paycheck has a stub, or apron, on which the employee can see his or her payroll itemization for that period. The only problem, in many cases, is that none of the terminology makes any sense to the person reading it. Terms like *FICA*, *SDI*, and *UI deductions* might as well be in Chinese for all the good they do. I've always wondered what people who design these information systems think about when they're designing them; it certainly can't be the person on the other end of the communication process.

I finally figured out why so many computer-generated items, like bank statements, customer accounts, paychecks, and accounting reports make so little sense to earthlings. They are set up by computer programers who know how to communicate with computers but not how to communicate with regular people. These folks inhabit their own particular world of process and terminology, and many of them lack the simplest social skills or skills of articulation. Many of them haven't the faintest idea how the mind of the "average person" processes information.

In many cases, technical people subject the customer to confusing, cryptic, jargon-packed messages without ever having tried the simple expedient of *testing them on a typical customer*. Why not hold up on finalizing the changes to the customer statement until we've shown it to a sample of 50 to 100 customers and asked them whether they understand it? Does it tell them what they need to know? Can they find out what they want quickly and conveniently? Does it overload them with information of no value or interest to them?

We will deal much more specifically with service system analysis in later chapters, but for this discussion it will help to recognize a very important point about the design of systems, policies, and procedures. For your own thinking processes, start thinking in terms of *customer-impact systems* and *customer-neutral systems*. This is a critical feature that deserves a great deal of attention.

A customer-impact system is one that directly or indirectly affects the customer at some moment of truth somewhere along the interface. The system that generates the bank statement, for example, is a customer-impact system. In terms of internal service, the purchase request system by which people activate the purchasing department is a customer-impact system. The employee performance appraisal system is a customer-impact system in that it affects the manager who has to use it. Customer-neutral systems are those that have no significant effect on the customer at any moment of truth. The distinction applies just as well to systems that affect internal customers as well as those that affect paying customers.

We should not have the right to design customer-impact systems without considering the impact, either direct or indirect, of those systems on the customer. That sounds like an unarguable point, but it happens constantly in almost all organizations.

The financial analysis department says, "We are going to require people who request analyses to submit their requests on a standard form. They'll have to spell out the problem they want analyzed, the time frame, contact person, and budget constraints. We won't honor requests unless they come in on these forms." They have just created a customer-impact system.

Where do they get off dictating to their customers how they shall bring their business? What right do they have to impose, unilaterally, these kinds of bureaucratic restrictions on their customers? This is bureaucratic thinking at its essence, and it is the enemy of service quality. Yet how can the department solve its need to organize and prioritize its customer requests? There are much better ways, as we shall see in later chapters.

TURF PROBLEMS: BORDERS AND BATTLES

One of the most pernicious influences on the quality of internal service, and a sure sign of lack of direction and misalignment of resources on the part of internal departments, is the outbreak of "turf" wars. According to Edwin T. Crego, Jr., head of service management programs at the Chicago-based consulting firm of Laventhol & Horwath, "Many support-department managers profess to be interested in serving their internal customers, but we often find they are really operating to a hidden bureaucratic agenda. They often have certain covert priorities of their own which may have little to do with service."

According to Crego, some of the priorities on the hidden bureaucratic agenda are:

- Increasing the number of employees under their control.
- Increasing their budget allocations.
- Positioning themselves as close to the chief executive as they can.
- Maximizing their influence on major decision processes.
- Gaining maximum latitude for action, independent of the wishes of the other departments.

In this kind of situation, excellent service may come about more by accident than by design. The turf wars tend to sap so much organizational energy that they leave very little for the service mission. An executive of a major publishing company once lamented to me, "You know, if we could only redirect some of this interdepartmental hostility outward at the competition, we could probably blow them away. Half the time we defeat ourselves before we ever get out on the battle field."

Organizational turf battles usually arise from just a few basic causes, all of which trace back to top management leadership. Sometimes the problem is an organizational structure that just doesn't work and throws people into cross-purposes against their will. In other situations, one or more selfish managers bent on self-aggrandizement get away with organizational games and draw the others into the same kinds of interactions.

Another common reason for turf battles is the lack of a clear company direction, which causes internal managers to be confused about the roles and contributions of their departments. And, of course, turf battles can also arise as a result of a "rat-race" environment created by the chief executive, who likes to keep his managers fighting with one another so they can't turn on him.

Whatever the cause, turf wars can be highly destructive to an internal service department. They can lead to bitter power struggles, hard feelings, and vengeful behavior that prevents everybody from giving the proper attention and effort to the quality of service, both internal and external. The chief executive has the responsibility for intervening in turf wars, tracking down and removing their causes, and helping people to work together for the common cause of service excellence.

FIEFDOMS: THE SEVEN SINS OF INTERNAL SERVICE

In *At America's Service,* I introduced a list of the "Seven Sins of Service," which are the most common ways in which unsuccessful service businesses antagonize their customers. Those seven sins, perpetrated at the customer interface, are Apathy, the Brush-Off, Coldness, Condescension, Robotism, the Rule Book, and the Runaround.

In the same way that many service businesses sin against their customers on a fairly regular basis, so do many internal service departments sin against their organizational customers. A "sinful" service department tends to subject its customers to one or more of these *seven sins of internal service*:

THE SEVEN SINS OF INTERNAL SERVICE

1. *The Black Hole:* Things go in but nothing ever seems to come out. Requests for information, advice, pleas for special assistance, requests to expedite processes all seem to go unheeded. The department seems to operate on its own self-motivated priorities and virtually ignores special requests from anybody—except, usually, senior management or somebody else who can put the heat on.

2. *The Bounce-Back:* The department seems to make a

hobby out of rejecting requests for service on procedural grounds. "You didn't fill in line 24 of the standard Service Request Form." "We are returning your request without action because you failed to provide a budget number." Instead of calling up the customer department to get the missing information, they self-righteously reject the request and throw it back in the needing department's face.

3. The Edict: Some departments seem to enjoy making declarations of what they will or won't do in the future. "Effective today, this department will no longer process budget requests unless they are accompanied by a written justification, signed by the unit supervisor." The message is, "This is how it's going to be; you can take it or leave it."

4. The Gotcha: Some departments have the type of functional responsibility that puts them in a position of surveillance over others. In such cases, they may get carried away with their policing roles. They seem to take sadistic pleasure in catching people in other departments making mistakes or violating the rules. Internal audit departments, legal departments, and affirmative action departments often fall into this kind of role distortion and adversarial mentality.

5. No-ism: Some departments tend to be "yes" departments, and others tend to be "no" departments. A "no" department is one that seems to enjoy exercising its veto power. The folks there like to say no more often than they say yes. Instead of a "can-do" attitude, they have a "no, you can't" attitude. They always seem to be telling their customers why something can't be done instead of looking for ways to meet their legitimate needs.

6. The Papermill: This is the department that likes to bury you in paperwork every time you try to get something done. They've got forms and special requests for everything you can think of. They've long since forgotten how to discuss a problem over the phone and take immediate action. Now everything has to be submitted on their standard form in triplicate with fifteen signatures before they'll even decide whether to say yes or no to it.

7. Turfism: Turfism is a jealous preoccupation with one's assigned area of responsibility, to the exclusion of common sense and compromise in the name of getting results. A "turf-ist" department is always poised for the attack, just in case somebody gets the idea that they can try to do something on their own or take unilateral action on some issue. All departments must look after their missions, of course, but it is not uncommon to see a turfist department head ignoring the needs of the customers and then jumping on them for trying to fulfill those needs by their own initiative.

One good place to start in assessing your organization's internal service orientation is to examine the various departments' attitudes toward one another. Which departments have earned reputations as sinful operations in the eyes of their customers? Which ones make it a point to avoid sinning against their customers, and find ways to add value to what they offer rather than detract from it?

SERVICE BARRIERS: EGOS AND ATTITUDES

It is not at all uncommon for internal support departments to project attitudes toward other departments that create barriers to service. In many organizations, the departments have become "compartments," with each one trying to do its own thing, put itself above the others, and feel superior. It's remarkable the extent to which departmental self-importance can go and the amount of animosity and antagonism it can generate.

Some departments with so-called policing functions can get so taken with themselves and so arrogant in their dealings with other departments that their internal customers ignore them or try to go around them to get their needs met. In one aerospace organization I worked with, the finance department had managed to achieve a death-grip on the process of pricing outgoing proposals intended to land new contracts. Pricing should be a marketing function, not a finance function, but a very conservative, risk-averse senior management always deferred to the finance people.

The company lost more than one competitive contract because the finance department, lacking the technical expertise to understand the proposed project, simply padded the estimate for safekeeping and put the price up beyond a winning level.

In one major automotive organization I worked with, the personnel department was so difficult to deal with and so determined that things were going to be done its way that it earned the nickname "the antipersonnel department." Managers all over the organization considered the department an obstacle to accomplishing anything and felt that its policies and practices were actually opposed to the humane employment and development of people.

Sometimes a department gets the reputation of being a "no" organization. Every answer it gives to a request for help or cooperation seems to be no. "Can you loan us some people to help us get this project completed on schedule?" "No." "Do you think we can expedite this process and eliminate the red tape, just this one time?" "No." "Can you give us an early look at the results of your study, before the final report comes out, so we can begin to get ready for the changes?" "No." Everything seems to be no, no, no. It's as if they enjoy saying it. Maybe they enjoy making other people frustrated or uncomfortable. Maybe they enjoy wielding their ceremonial "no" power.

This tends to happen especially when there is no clear sense of company mission and no clear commitment to quality service. Without a strong and unitary message from the top of the organization, the internal departments often drift into these kinds of self-important, adversarial attitudes toward one another. Asserting power becomes more important than giving service. Blaming becomes more important than solving problems.

Internal service departments ought to be "yes" organizations. They should be willing to stretch themselves, adapt their processes, and make special efforts for the customers they have to serve. This style of operating comes from a strong service culture and a strong middle manager. Both are necessary for internal teamwork and cooperation to be at its best.

RESTRUCTURING FOR SERVICE

Just as internal service organizations can cripple themselves with their systems, policies, and procedures, so can they cripple themselves with organization charts that don't make sense in terms of service quality. Many support departments structure themselves for their own convenience rather than for the convenience of their customers. They may then take it upon themselves to try to force their customers to deal with them at their convenience.

This is a critical point, which deserves some careful thinking. We may ask: When the convenience of the customer comes into conflict with the convenience of the department, which of the two interests deserves higher priority? One would think the customer interest should come first in most cases, i.e., that the department should learn to adapt, sacrifice, or modify its approach to make sure the service quality is at its highest. Yet how many support departments have rules about what they will and won't do for the customer?

How many departments simply refuse to expedite certain customer actions on the flimsy pretext that "it would set a bad precedent. We'd have to do it for everybody." Well, *why not* do it for everybody? When someone in a support department says, "No, we can't do that for you. We're not set up for that," well, maybe they *should* be set up for that. And if a lot of people want it that way, maybe that's evidence that they should learn to do it that way.

Should a service department consider changing its very structure in the name of quality service to its customers? In some cases, the answer is absolutely yes. In many cases there will be trade-offs, and the department has to use its resources as wisely as possible. But I don't think we should ever reject out of hand any plausible approach to structuring that promises better service within the parameters of good business.

One of the structural issues that comes up often in large organizations is the centralization versus decentralization issue, which often takes the form of an interdepartmental turf issue. In some organizations, the operating units become progressively exasperated with, say, the training department for its lack of responsiveness to their needs. They go to top management and sell the idea that training should be decentralized, i.e., that each of the major operating divisions should handle its own training, at least on an operational basis. They're willing to let the central training department handle all the other stuff, such as equal opportunity training, safety, basic supervision, and everything else they don't really care about.

Some organizations go through this centralization-decentralization agony every few years like a pendulum. Neither way works very well, largely because of other bigger problems, and they keep shifting back and forth. Meanwhile, the original service they were trying to improve is still lousy, and the customers still go begging.

THE SPOC: SINGLE POINT OF CONTACT

Another organizational issue that often arises in support departments is the generalist versus specialist issue. This happens particularly in cases where the service requires considerable expertise on the part of the employee who handles the matter, as in computer departments, personnel departments, legal departments, and groups that do special analyses. One school of thought says the department should appoint one or more generalists to handle all matters with the customer department. This generalist should work with the various specialists to organize the resources to solve the customer's problem. This is the so-called SPOC approach, i.e., single point of contact.

Many large computer departments have moved toward the SPOC approach over the past 10 years with a function usually called the information center. This is a small staff of people who serve in a liaison capacity with nontechnical consumers of their service. They are usually selected for their ability to talk plainly to earthlings as well as for their general knowledge of data processing solutions.

The opposing school of thought says that individual specialists can best take care of the customer's needs on a case-by-case basis. They argue that the SPOC can't know all of the various specialties involved and will usually have to hand the matter off to a specialist anyway. Why have a go-between involved when the customer could just as well deal with the specialist directly? Also, they argue, some customers don't like having a go-between person screen them from contact with the individual experts they have come to know and trust. When a manager wants to talk to a particular specialist he or she has worked with before, why should the manager have to make the approach through a third party?

Both have their advantages and disadvantages. Is there a way to resolve the dilemma? How do we settle the matter? We settle it by asking the basic question: What's best for the customer in this particular case? In my view, the service department should be willing to operate in a way that may be somewhat less convenient for itself if it is more convenient for the customer.

In some cases, a SPOC might make more sense than the many-to-many type of interface. In other cases, multiple contacts may work better. But in the end, we should make the choice in favor of service quality, not in favor of the personal preferences of the people in the service department.

The same holds true for virtually all structural issues. If we don't inject the service-quality factor early into the analysis, we run the risk of designing an organizational structure that looks good on paper and feels good to the people working within it but does a lousy job of looking after the customers' needs. The customer interface should get primary consideration in any treatment of organizational structure.

CHAPTER 4

THE MIDDLE MANAGEMENT LEADERSHIP CRISIS

Advice to the bureaucrat: when in charge, delegate; when in doubt, ponder; when in trouble, mumble.

—*Charles Boren*

MIDDLE MANAGEMENT: A NO-WIN JOB

Middle managers may be the least understood species in the entire organizational menagerie. As a segment of working society, they have come in for more criticism, more blame, and more scorn in recent years than any other. They seem to fulfill some bizarre need we have for someone to persecute for the failings of large organizations.

Many books and articles have appeared in the management literature about "the middle management problem." This phrase generally means that middle managers act too bureaucratically, resist change, stifle innovation, and impede top-to-bottom communications. Executives and frontline people alike, as well as management authors, seem equally exasperated with what they see as the failure of middle managers, in general, to provide leadership, inspiration, and change management.

Pejorative terms abound for describing middle managers. Some Scandinavian executives call them "the rock-wool layer," meaning that they're like a fuzzy layer of insulation between upper and lower levels of the organization, preventing ideas and information from flowing in either direction. The British call them "the damp layer," suggesting that they water down and cool down all the exciting ideas that come their way. Americans tend to call them simply "the bureaucracy."

Some organizational theorists are calling for the elimination of middle managers, almost as if by surgery. The reasoning goes: if an organ is not doing its job, cut it out. Some are predicting that the proliferation of computers and the increasingly knowledge-intensive nature of organizations will solve the problem naturally. Eventually it will be only the senior executives, the frontline workers, maybe some supervisors, and a whole bunch of computers and networks. Information and ideas will flow freely, and the whole organization will be much more dynamic.

All of these approaches suffer from a certain amount of naiveté, I believe. Sweeping generalizations about the new organizational structures of the future are fun but often unfounded. In large, complex organizations, it will always be necessary to subdivide resources along functional lines, and it will always be necessary to focus responsibility at certain key points. It is true, I believe, that many organizations could function better with fewer management layers than they have, but I'm not in favor of simply ripping out layers of management to try to solve "the middle-management problem." As Peter Drucker has noted, "Reorganization is tantamount to surgery. One doesn't just cut."

By the way, who are these middle managers that are causing such problems? Do you know any? What do they look like? How do they walk and talk? What do they do? It's interesting to talk to an actual middle manager about middle management. I've done this quite a few times in the last few years, and I've found the conversations that have ensued quite enlightening.

Often I'll meet someone who tells me he or she is "head of such-and-such a department." "Oh," I'll respond. "Are you a middle manager?" Usually the answer is "Uh, well, yes." Then a conversation develops around the problems of handling a middle management job. At some point I like to ask, "Tell me— since so many people talk about middle managers as obstacles, or as bureaucrats—do you see yourself as a bureaucrat?" This usually draws a somewhat startled disclaimer. "Are you a bureaucrat, in your opinion?" I ask. "No, I wouldn't say I'm a bureaucrat or an obstacle," is the usual answer. "So you don't see yourself as a 'problem,'" I ask. "No, I'm not a problem. The system is the problem. If I had it my way, things would work a lot differently. But I don't have it my way. I have to follow the policies they give me."

So we have a curious state of affairs. We have the widespread perception that middle managers are obstacles to change, and yet we have great difficulty finding middle managers who will plead guilty to the charge. There seems to be an assumption that competent people who have succeeded as first-line supervisors and tactical managers suddenly become dense, dull witted, narrow minded, and recalcitrant immediately upon promotion to middle management jobs.

Something doesn't quite compute. It makes more sense to think of the problem not as a problem with middle managers but as a problem with middle management. In other words, it's a problem of role definition and role effectiveness.

It seems to me that a middle-management job in many organizations, especially large ones, is a no-win deal. Middle managers feel themselves hemmed in by policies, procedures, and rules of someone else's making, and at the same time they feel themselves under pressure to innovate, communicate, and manage change. They feel pressure from the top and demands from the bottom. They typically have less latitude for action than onlookers seem to think they have, or at least they perceive themselves as having less.

In my view, we do not need a way to get rid of middle managers, because we need them. We need a way to enfranchise them as leaders. This, I believe, is what the internal service concept can do. If this turns out to be true, it may be one of the most important impacts on the practice of management ever to come along.

ROLES, GOALS, AND CONFUSION

I have contended that the "middle management problem" is really a problem of role confusion, not a problem of incompetence.

If this is so, the solution must come through role clarification, not through recrimination and persecution. We have to understand the dilemma many middle managers find themselves in, and we have to help them find ways out of that dilemma.

Most middle managers have "no-go power," but no "go power." That is to say, they are usually in the position of approving or disapproving—no-go power—but they can seldom originate things—go power. This is typically a fact of organizational structures and the division of authority. Nothing we can say here applies to 100 percent of middle managers, of course, but it seems to be true that most of them have been created as functionaries rather than as leaders.

One cynic referred to this passive gatekeeping role as "merely that of a coordinator, not a leader. All a coordinator can do," he complained, "is point with pride and view with alarm." In many respects this holds true, and many middle managers seem to feel their roles confine them to this kind of reactive administrating.

In addition to getting pressure and criticism from both top and bottom levels, the middle manager often faces another psychological barrier to assuming a strong leadership role. This comes in the form of a "we don't need you" type of message from the people at the tactical levels who see initiatives from middle management as a form of interference in their day-to-day work activities. In truth, the middle manager is often removed, by the very nature of his or her role, from direct contact with the work activities. It takes a direct act of intervention to get involved. This is different from the role of the tactical supervisor, who is deeply involved in the work of the unit whether he or she wants to be or not.

Most multilevel organizational structures tend to have a naturally occurring alternation of *tactical* and *administrative* levels as you go from the front line to the very top. The floor nurses are tactical; the head nurse handles the paperwork. The departmental nursing director is more tactical than administrative; the head of nursing is an administrator. This phenomenon seems to occur in virtually all organizations as a result of the way we group resources and assign responsibilities.

In most organizations you will find more dissatisfaction

with individuals at administrative levels than with those at tactical levels. It seems to be in the nature of things.

Further, a supervisor who graduates from a tactical level to his or her first administrative job will typically have difficulty adjusting to the new role. Tactical management experience, it seems clear, does not prepare one particularly well for an administrative kind of job. The work of the administrator tends to be more abstract, more cerebral, more informational, less interpersonal, and less "hands-on." Whereas before the manager dealt directly with the problems and processes of the work itself, now he or she is dealing with the problems and processes of the organization.

Let's look at the situations of several typical middle managers in typical service organizations. Fred M is a district manager for a chain of drugstores. He has 11 store managers reporting to him, each responsible for in the neighborhood of $1 million in yearly sales. The company's philosophy calls for maximum independence and autonomy on the part of the store manager. The manager exercises great latitude in choosing products for inventory, setting up advertising and promotion, and certainly in hiring and placement of staff. *Question:* What is Fred's job?

Fred's job, to quote the unnamed cynic, is largely to "point with pride and view with alarm." Ask him what his role is, and he will tell you it is to make sure the store managers meet their performance goals. He checks on their progress, visits their stores regularly, inspects the operations, and zeroes in on any problem that needs fixing.

Ask any of the store managers what Fred's role is, and they will probably give you a blank look and say something like, "He's the district manager." Now, Fred may be very competent and he may take a very imaginative approach to his job, but the majority of Freds in the company have fallen comfortably into this "inspector" role. Whenever he comes around, the assumption at the local level is that something is wrong or that he's just "checking up."

Seldom does he come around with a new idea or a different strategy for building sales. He's just doing his job as a district manager.

Take another example, Maxine R, who is head of the respiratory therapy department at a major hospital. She was an outstanding respiratory therapist, and then she got promoted to head of the department. She has three teams of respiratory therapists and technicians reporting to her, plus several specialists who deal with the special needs of certain doctors and their customers (i.e., patients). Each therapy team works under the guidance of a lead therapist, who is responsible for covering all of the day's projects, dealing with physicians, keeping the equipment in good working order, working with difficult patients, and keeping the others working well as a team. *Question:* What is Maxine supposed to be doing?

Maxine's job is to "keep the department running." She prepares the budget, locates qualified people to fill the open vacancies, works out the daily schedules for the various teams and projects, attends staff meetings, and reviews the performance of the various service groups in the department. Ask Maxine what she does, and she'll probably say, "I'm the department head." Ask one of the staff what she does, and that person will probably say something like, "She handles the paperwork," or "She keeps track of the rest of us," or "She's the one who handles the money."

A third example: Jake P is the head of a financial services unit within the finance division of a gas and electric company. Jake has several key units reporting to him: treasury operations, cash management, and financial analysis. Treasury handles the actual assets of the company, including the vault, stock and bond safekeeping, and daily cash operations. Cash management has the mission of investing the company's available cash on a daily basis to maximize the return on liquid assets. And financial analysis is a group that conducts specialized financial and economic studies on an on-call basis for various executive departments of the company. *Question:* What is Jake's job?

Jake's job is to "tie everything together." He oversees three distinctly different work groups, each with its own individual activities, issues, and problems. Each of the groups has a well-qualified supervisor who understands his or her responsibilities fairly clearly. Can you get a sense of how Jake feels when he deals with these various groups or their leaders? It's as if they all have their marching orders, they know what they are supposed to do, and they don't need much "management." Whenever Jake tries to get involved, they tend to give him quizzical looks, as if to say, "What do *you* want? We're taking care of everything. Don't bother us."

Jake feels like a fifth wheel. So do Maxine and Fred. All of them feel they are making a contribution, of course, but none of them feels really close to the work. The deployment of resources places them in an overseeing role rather than a direct-involvement role. This is the fundamental nature of a middle management job.

In most organizations, probably the vast majority, middle managers slip quietly and comfortably into these passive gate-keeping roles, often with no thought at all for alternative approaches. Most of us human beings are quite malleable. Whether we like to admit it or not, most of us tend to take on the mind-sets and habit patterns of the roles in which we find ourselves. If the nature of the role suggests coordination, we become coordinators. If it suggests budgeting and resource allocation, we become budgeteers. If it suggests approving and vetoing, we learn the thumbs-up and thumbs-down responses and often little else.

Middle managers in any organization are typically reflections of the prevailing organizational culture. In a company culture that is risk averse, rule based, and ritualistic, they tend to become risk averse, rule based, and ritualistic. Bureaucracy begets bureaucracy. The style and attitudes of the chief executive often have a big influence on the habits of the middle managers. If the top person is a caretaker, you tend to get caretaker management. If he or she is a bureaucrat, you tend to get bureaucrats. There often tends to be a "cloning" effect, in which the middle-level managers project the kinds of managerial styles they believe the chief wants to see. In some cases the chief executive himself is little more than a middle manager with nobody above him.

Perhaps there really is no role confusion, or at least there is very little. Maybe most middle managers really do understand their roles pretty well. The problem may be that everyone around them is wanting them to live up to different roles, roles which do not exist within the culture of the organization. Maybe we put middle managers into administrating roles and then want them to be leaders. When they react as administrators, we want to blame them for having become incompetent, for having failed at leadership, or perhaps for just not caring.

Instead, what we have to do is get a clearer understanding of what middle managers can do, what kinds of roles they can play, and what kinds of contributions the organization needs from them. Only then can we help them recast their roles as leaders and enablers.

THE "INVISIBLE COMPETITOR"

Sometimes people in internal service departments develop the attitude over time that they are "the only game in town" and that the various customer departments really have no choice but to come to them for their services. Some of them even become highhanded and cavalier about it, projecting a "take it or leave it" attitude toward those who complain about the way they operate. They see themselves as having no competition, in the sense that customer departments do not have authority—in most cases—to go outside the organization and hire the services on the free market. For this reason, they feel no pressure to be customer oriented or to put their customers' needs first.

The unfortunate fact, though, is that they do have "competitors" in a sense, and their customers may be patronizing these competitors on a regular basis. Their competitors are "invisible," but they do exist. Let's explore that notion a bit further. Perhaps a case example will make the point most clearly.

Years ago, when I was new to the consulting business, I received a request from a middle-sized firm to develop a special program for them aimed at improving the win rate of their proposals to government agencies for contract work. They specialized in data management, which is the production of technical manuals, system documentation, and various paper-oriented reference systems.

The project included an intensive seminar program lasting

five full days, in which we trained their key project leaders in the techniques of proposal-based marketing. One afternoon, during a break in the seminar program, I chatted with the division manager who had conceived of the project and who had engaged me to do the work. I asked, "Do you have a training department in the company?" "Yes, we do," he replied, with no further elaboration.

I asked, "Why aren't they involved in this project, since it's largely a training activity?" He smiled a bit sardonically and said simply, "Not qualified." When I pressed him further, he told me he considered dealing with the training department a waste of his time and that he had better options for solving his problems. Presumably these options included engaging outside consultants to design and implement training programs. In this particular case, the training people apparently hadn't put up a fuss of any kind. They were accustomed to having managers exclude them from their plans and go around them to get their needs met.

It was clear to me that the training department in this case did indeed have "competition." And the competitor wasn't only I or firms like mine. The competitor was the manager. Every time the manager took some alternative route to get a solution that he should have had a right to expect from the training department, he was competing with them for their business. The company was spending resources over and above those of the training department to get its training needs met.

Many times over the years I've seen this kind of "invisible competition" going on in organizations. When managers can't get what they need from the data processing department, they buy personal computers and hire staff to develop software for them. When the personnel department can't provide good management development programs, the executives hire consultants to do it for them.

Who knows how much money is wasted in large organizations as a result of this invisible competition effect? How many internal departments are creating competition for themselves by failing to recognize and meet the real needs of their customers? If we're looking for ways to make organizations more productive and more efficient in their use of resources, it would seem that making service departments more responsive to their customers' needs would be a good place to start.

THE CRYING NEED FOR LEADERSHIP IN SERVICE BUSINESSES

According to noted management theorist, consultant, and university professor Dr. Warren Bennis,

"Today's employee is overmanaged and underled."

Bennis is using the term *managed* in the connotation of *administrated*. In other words, his work shows there is an almost universal desire in business organizations to set up a *system* for running things and to let the system direct the people. This is in contrast to what he believes is a crying need for personal, one-to-one, face-to-face leadership.

Service businesses are especially susceptible to the side effects of this administrative mind-set, because service excellence depends far more on *individual excellence* than is the case in manufacturing organizations. At the customer interface, the employee *is* the product or at the very least is a key part of the product.

In a manufacturing setting, one carburetor or chocolate bar or color television is just about the same as another. But in a service setting, one moment of truth is never exactly like another. Each has its own distinctive drama, because each takes place with a different human being as the customer. Individual excellence in these cases, as we have known for many years, results from the cooperation of an employee with the right potential and a leader who can invite and encourage that potential.

This desire to enfranchise middle managers as leaders is becoming a critical organizational issue. It is rapidly growing stronger in many businesses and many countries. We will surely see a greater concentration on middle-management roles and responsibilities as the service revolution continues to develop. We will almost certainly see a resurgence in leadership training, possibly at all levels of organizations and particularly at middle-management levels.

One example that will bear watching is SAS' Leadership College, launched by Jan Carlzon in 1988. At the urging of Jan Lapidoth, Carlzon's chief architect of cultural change, he commissioned a study of leadership principles applicable to service businesses. The result was the creation of an intensive training program that extends over a number of months and aims to reinforce key skills and behaviors in managers who attend.

According to Jan Lapidoth of the Leadership School, "We're attempting to bring about a revolution in managerial thinking. We have to contradict and counteract some of the beliefs and conclusions they have reached in their early managerial training and in their experience. We want to reorient them to think as leaders, not as administrators." It is likely that every single SAS manager will at some time go through this special leadership training.

Carlzon, in true visionary fashion, looked ahead to the future of the "new SAS" and wasn't exactly happy with everything he thought he saw. Part of what he didn't like was what he perceived as a resurgence of rigidity and bureaucratic thinking in the company:

> In the early days of the turnaround, things were in chaos; just about everything was in an uproar. But it was exciting. People knew that big new things were coming. They felt part of a big adventure. The "law-and-order" types who had dominated the culture in years past had to take a back seat to the "chaos" types.
>
> Now, however, after a number of years of experience with the cultural revolution, we still haven't solved all of the problems we want to solve, but the pendulum is starting to swing back toward law and order again. I can't say I like it.

Carlzon is facing some fairly fundamental cultural issues. Success tends to create its own special types of problems. SAS is still a very successful travel service company, but there seem to be internal stresses and strains arising that may signal the end of the first major wave of the revolution. What will come next is open to conjecture, but, whatever it is, it will almost surely involve an attempt by Carlzon to reorient the managerial culture to a leadership culture.

This, I believe, is a natural outcome of a shift from manufacturing management to service management, which is what SAS is going through. It seems to me, all in all, to be a healthy and needed next stage. Even though the near-term effects may be somewhat destabilizing and confusing to many people, it is a logical extension of the revolution Carlzon and his management team started in 1980 to 1981. Characteristic of Carlzon's approach to cultural evolution is his willingness to invest surprising levels of resources in areas that traditional "Harvard Business School" management would never recognize as worthwhile.

For example, he was one of the first executives to use 100 percent "wall-to-wall" training to order to communicate the service message to every SAS employee. He is likely to make a substantial investment in leadership development as well, because he believes it to be absolutely essential to carrying the revolution forward.

It is an interesting exercise of the mind to try to place SAS at the present time along some imaginary continuum of cultural development, i.e., the "natural" phases of its cultural revolution. We don't really know what those phases are, so we'll have to invent them here for the sake of discussion. It seems to me, extrapolating from the SAS experience and observing a number of other major service organizations in their progress toward a wholly new culture, that the revolution from the manufacturing management model to the service management model will unfold in approximately three stages:

1. The customer-consciousness revolution.
2. The systems revolution.
3. The leadership revolution.

Most, if not all, service businesses seem to begin with the customer-consciousness revolution. There must be a wholesale redirection of people's attention from activities to outcomes.

They first need to begin thinking in terms of the customer, the customer interface, and the moments of truth that make up the interface. This is where SAS began, and it seems to be the natural starting point as executives try to get their organizations going down the path of service excellence. Many organizations never complete this first stage of the revolution; many more never go beyond it.

The second revolution is usually the systems revolution. This is the stage of getting serious about the means and methods of service. This is where organizations begin to take a close look at customer-impact systems, facilities, policies, procedures, skills training, and all the rest of the operational matters that call for attention if there is ever going to be a follow-through on the vision of service. This is usually the stage where executives feel most gratified about concrete results.

The third revolution, the leadership revolution, is largely speculative at this point. It is probably the most difficult stage to navigate. Certainly most of the organizations whose executives get excited about service do not reach this level, although they may experience some sense of it. This stage of the revolution, if it unfolds, causes executives and managers to think about their roles, the business, and the people in new ways.

If this so-called leadership revolution turns out to be anything more than a figment of my imagination, it will be a most interesting phenomenon indeed. It will not take place spontaneously; it will require a great deal of effort and intellectual leadership on the part of a number of senior corporate executives who want to see it happen. It will require a large input of resources, and it will take time. It will challenge the very conceptual basis of western management as we have learned it over the past 40 years or so.

But in any case, it is already clear that organizations of all kinds, not just service businesses, are desperately in need of more and better leadership on the part of internal managers. The so-called middle management problem is really a need and a desire for leadership on the part of middle managers. As mentioned, the internal service concept holds a great deal of promise for calling forth this new type of leadership and for enabling middle managers to rethink their roles, contributions, and results.

THE INTERNAL SERVICE MODEL: A WAY OUT OF THE WOODS

Let's try to paint a picture of the solution to the middle management problem, seen through the framework of the internal service approach. In following chapters I will suggest a step-by-step method of attack on the problem of middle management role confusion. I will offer a recipe of sorts, which virtually any manager can use to establish a clear direction for his or her organization. For this discussion, let's examine the broad outlines of the solution in organizational terms.

Three things have to happen for middle managers to become the kinds of service leaders needed by their organizations and their people: (1) They have to adopt a new mind-set about themselves and their roles. (2) They have to think through the roles of their organizations in the context of the goals of the overall business of which they are a part. (3) They need to have the support of a service-oriented organizational culture around and above them. Let's examine those three prerequisites.

First comes a new mind-set. The old mind-set is one of administration, of procedure, of approval and disapproval, of passively reacting to events and problems presented by others. The new mind-set must be a proactive one. It must be entrepreneurial in its focus. It must be broader in its scope. And it must be much more business focused than in the past. This will require some careful teaching and development of middle managers. Some of them currently operate this way already, but by no means most. Managers will have to learn this new mind-set, and that will take some impetus from the leaders above them. As more and more of them learn and adopt it, it may well become contagious. Good role models can serve to project the possibilities to others better than anything else.

Next comes a complete rethinking of what the manager's department or unit is all about. Succeeding chapters will have a great deal to say about this process. For this discussion let us note that the manager of an internal department, or for that matter the manager of a customer-contact department, must go through roughly the same reasoning process on behalf of the department that the senior executives have to go through for the whole company. He or she must think through what the department's contribution is to the whole organization, how to express that contribution in terms of a service mission, how to teach and dramatize that mission to all of the people working in the department, and how to align or realign resources to those ends, and especially how to measure and evaluate the quality of that contribution.

And finally, senior management must provide the inspiration, the reasons, and the motivation for the middle manager to operate with this new mind-set and this new plan of attack. The more fully and publicly committed to service quality the chief executive, the more the managers will respond by giving direction to their people in terms of service quality. The service culture is the indispensable soil within which the commitment to entrepreneurial leadership can take root. It must operate as a reinforcing environment, expecting, inviting, and rewarding managers to provide the kind of proactive, nonbureaucratic, personal leadership their organizations need.

Putting these three causal factors together—a new mind-set, a new plan of attack, and a reinforcing service culture—is not an easy task, by any means. But it is most definitely possible. And by breaking it down into its essential components and making it a teachable methodology, I hope to show that determined executives and well-intentioned middle managers can team up to bring it about.

CHAPTER 5

MOVING TOWARD AN
INTERNAL SERVICE CULTURE

Take care of the means, and the end will take care of itself.

—Gandhi

WHAT IS A SERVICE CULTURE?

One of the simplest definitions of *organizational culture* is contributed by Terrence Deal and Allan Kennedy in their book *Corporate Cultures*. They call it "the way we do things around here." A *service culture* is a way of doing things that places a high value on service quality because of its crucial role in the success of the business.[1]

I sometimes use a somewhat more technical definition of culture in discussing organizational change management:

A culture is a social context that influences the ways people behave and relate.

This says the very same thing as the Deal-Kennedy definition, with an emphasis on the elements we have to focus on if we want to change or influence that culture. We can elaborate the definition even further with respect to service by saying that a service culture is a social context *based on quality of service* that operates to influence people's working behavior and working relationships in such a way that they work toward the common value of excellent service.

A service culture comes into being as a result of the interplay of a number of forces, the strongest of which is probably the influence of the chief executive and his or her senior executives. The nature of the organization's business environment and the competitive habit patterns of the players in that environment also provide an impetus. And, certainly, the national-social culture of the people who make up the work force has a strong influence. All of these factors, ideally, come together to create a very high individual and collective commitment to outstanding service as a central value for the survival and prosperity of the business.

How do you recognize a service culture when you see one? Here are some of the hallmarks:

1. There is a clear vision or concept for service.
2. Executives constantly preach and teach the service gospel.
3. Managers model customer-first behavior.
4. Quality service is expected of everyone.
5. Quality service is rewarded.

Everything starts with the vision. Top management has studied the organization's business environment and formed a clear idea of what it has to be and do in the eyes of the customer in order to get his business. This vision, or *service strategy* as I have called it in the theory of service management, is more than a platitude. It is a direction in which to march. It spells out the special nature of the organization's service offering and shows how that special approach will meet with approval in at least some segment of the marketplace. It is simple but not trivial. It is dramatic but not fanciful. It is achievable but not mundane. In particular, it is teachable and preachable. It is, in short, the organizing principle for an attack on the market based on service quality.

The executives constantly teach and preach the service vision because they know that nothing will happen if they simply write it down and put it into the file cabinet. It takes a lot of work to get all the people in an organization thinking about one single, big idea, but the work has to be done. When SAS launched its highly acclaimed turnaround program in 1980, president Jan Carlzon traveled all over Scandinavia, personally taking the message to the people at every business location.

"I took my message directly to the front line," he said. "I spent two thirds of my time for over a year and a half, just talking to the people about service and about my plan for the new SAS. I said it so many times I thought I would throw up if I had to say it once more. But that's exactly what I did. I just said it once more and once more and once more."

In a service culture, managers "walk their talk." They model customer-first behavior, and the employees see the congruence between what they say and what they do. This is a common problem in many organizations that have not yet come to terms with the level of commitment needed for outstanding service. Managers hope to gain great service by talking about it, but they don't act about it. Buck Rogers, in his book *The IBM Way*, illustrates the depth of commitment he and his mentor Tom Watson, Jr., had.[2]

According to Rogers, Watson had talked many times about the customer being the key to the business. On one occasion, Watson called a meeting on short notice. Rogers, at that time head of IBM's Data Processing Division, had been out of the office, meeting with one of his customers who was having a major problem. Watson didn't take kindly to Rogers' not getting to the meeting on time, so he held up the proceeding until Rogers arrived. By that time, it was early evening, several hours after the meeting was supposed to start. All the other executives were sitting impatiently, waiting for Rogers.

When Rogers walked in, Watson jumped all over him for not getting to the meeting at the prescribed time. Rogers looked the old man in the eye and reminded him of his own dictum: The customer comes first. Watson acceded sheepishly and started the meeting.

The next important characteristic of service culture, the all-pervasive expectation of quality service, has to be "part of the woodwork." People in frontline jobs, whether they serve the paying customers or the internal customers, will come up to meet whatever expectations their leaders place upon them. If they receive the service quality message as a fundamental part of their indoctrination briefing when they first hire into their jobs, they begin to take it seriously. If they hear their supervisors talk about service quality and the customer-first way of doing things, they begin to see it as part of their reality. When their bosses hear it from *their* bosses, they can tell that it works at all levels.

When they see their jobs in the context of the company's overall performance, they realize that they play an important role, and they feel responsible to meet the expectations of that role. When they see their more experienced co-workers committed to doing right by the customer, they take a lesson from that role modeling. In short, all of the signals coming from their work environment—the service culture—tell them that their bosses and co-workers, as well as their customers, expect the best from them.

And finally, one of the most important elements of a service culture is the means for rewarding and reinforcing people for delivering quality service. In a service culture there is a closed-loop system, either formal or informal, which senses and appreciates excellence. It's not phony or artificial. It's not statistical. It's not mechanical. It is genuine, honest, and appreciative. It is individual and personal.

Psychologist William James contended:

The deepest longing in every human being is the need to be appreciated.

Leaders in service cultures realize this and act on it every day.

LANGUAGE AND CUSTOMS: INDICATORS OF CULTURE

An intriguing aspect of business cultures that deserves much closer study than it receives is the *language* of the organization—the verbal environment that surrounds and interpenetrates the thinking of everybody working there. Just as you can get an idea of the things that an individual considers personally important by listening to what he or she says, you can do the same thing in an organization. By listening to the verbal processes of the business, you can understand how it operates and what its culture is, often more accurately than by asking the executives.

Language—the terminology, jargon, figures of speech, and metaphors people use every day—is a window into the collective unconscious of the organization and its culture. I find it fascinating to listen to the language context of a typical executive meeting or a work discussion among employees. In just a few minutes one can detect verbal cues that reveal attitudes about the customer, about work, about employees, about the executives, about the company, about the industry, and even about life itself.

For example, the presence or absence of the word *customer* in the conversation says a great deal about customer-consciousness. The frequency with which financial factors arise indicates attitudes about resources. Metaphors and figures of speech portray an accepted style of discourse. Heavy use of profanity, sexual humor, and male figures of speech tend to indicate a "macho" culture dominated by male values and attitudes.

Figures of speech relating to sports, warfare, and combat suggest a relatively aggressive set of attitudes, again often male in their origin. Extensive use of technical terminology indicates, of course, a technocratic culture.

Deliberately changing the terminology of the culture can have the effect of changing mind-sets, attitudes, and the focus of attention and consequently the substance of the culture itself to an extent. Jan Lapidoth of Scandinavian Airlines System says, "We used to fly airplanes. Now we fly people." It may sound like a cute rhetorical trick, but please reflect for a moment on what it conveys. Sure, you have to have the people, or it won't make sense to fly airplanes. But the old way of saying it causes various mental associations that put the thinker into a mind-set that is fundamentally mechanical and operational. The new way causes associations that lead to preoccupation with the people as individual human beings and customers, not as freight.

I was involved in an interesting analysis of terminology with respect to executive missions at a public utility. One executive expressed his perception of his mission by saying, "My mission is to look after some 2,000 miles of gas transmission pipeline." Another executive rejoined, "I disagree. I think your mission is to look after the *customers* who are connected to 2,000 miles of pipeline." It struck me as a small distinction verbally but an enormous one intellectually. The first executive, of course, agreed that the newer formulation was more valid.

Another very interesting aspect of language within business culture deals with the names people use in referring to their customers. In some types of business cultures, people seldom use the term *customer*. They have evolved special terms that define the customers from the point of view of what the organization does to or for them, rather than in terms of their roles as buyers or users of a service. In health care, for instance, the term *customer* is almost a form of obscenity. "We don't have customers; we have *patients*," is the usual comment. *Patient* is actually a very interesting term in itself. What does it convey? I believe it conveys a passive role for the customer. As a patient, you are supposed to be patient—to wait patiently until the all-knowing caregiver is ready to take your case. You are not a customer; you are not a buyer. You are a patient, a person in need. Whenever I work with hospitals, I have to warn the executives ahead of time that I generally refuse to use the term *patient*; I call them *customers*. The warning is necessary because they're likely to think I don't know the first thing about the health-care industry.

Have you ever considered some of the other specialized terms used by service businesses to avoid calling their customers *customers*? Public utilities like to call them *ratepayers*; that's their only role, to supply the money to operate the energy system. Think about that term for a moment: *ratepayer*. Do you think of yourself as a ratepayer? Or would you rather think of yourself as a customer who buys energy from the utility? I'm not suggesting the terminology should bother you to the point of inciting you to burn down the company's building, but it does telegraph a very definite perception about the customer. And perceptions predispose people to behave in certain ways.

I recently gave a service management seminar to the executives of a very large association. Two minutes into the session, when I used the term *customer*, one executive interrupted me to say, "Excuse me, but I'm not sure you understand our operation. We have *members*, not customers." When I contended that members are still customers, a lively discussion ensued. That point became a relatively important one for the organization, which, by the way, is known for giving excellent service to its members/customers.

Insurance companies like to call their customers *policyholders*. That's all they do; they hold policies. Banks call them *accountholders*, psychiatrists call them *clients*, and so on. It strikes me that virtually all of these special terms have one primary objective and benefit for the service provider, which is a dangerous one, in my view. They all have the effect of portraying the customer as passive and powerless. They all describe the customer in terms of how the service organization acts on the customer, not how the customer acts on the organization.

This makes it easy and convenient to shift the focus from the customer as principal actor to the service provider as principal actor. It's much more comfortable that way. But it may be a dangerous kind of a mind-set. I believe we need to keep the implications conveyed by the term *customer* very much in the minds of people who perform and manage service work. It may be all right to use special terminology to describe the consumer of the service, but not at the expense of misperceiving the priorities in the service relationship.

There is much more to this concept of language habits in relation to service culture, but for this discussion the point is that we need to understand the culture in its many dimensions if we hope to modify it and reorient it toward a commitment to service excellence.

THE INTERNAL SERVICE TRIANGLE

Now we can tie together everything said so far about the internal service concept to form a picture of the successful service organization. It has committed service employees who take their motivation and guidance from three elements of their surroundings:

1. The culture of the organization.
2. The leadership they experience.
3. The organizational structure.

Putting the employee at the center of the picture, we can represent internal service in terms of a model first introduced in *At America's Service*, which is the *internal service triangle*.[3]

Whereas the original service triangle model introduced in *Service America!*[4] showed the customer at the center with strategy, people, and systems revolving around him or her, now we need to zero in on one specific element of that triangle, which is the people. We need to build an internal service trian-

FIGURE 5–1
The Internal Service Triangle

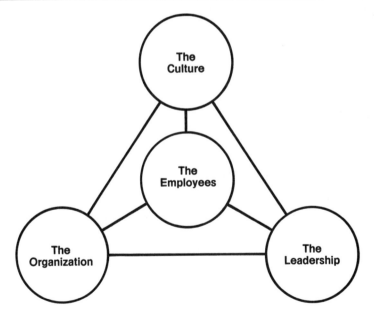

gle specifically around the service people to show how *they* are served.

The triangle of internal service suggests that the frontline employee needs support from all three sources: the culture, the leaders, and the organizational structure and systems. If all of these elements are properly aligned behind the employee, he or she can do the best job possible in rendering service, either to the paying customer or to the internal customer.

The preceding discussion in this chapter has dealt with the middle management leadership crisis and suggested a way out of it. It has dealt with organizational craziness and suggested a way to cure it. And it has dealt with the need for a service-based culture and suggested what it has to look like.

The remainder of this book deals with the how—how to enfranchise managers as leaders, how to build and reinforce the culture, and how to make the systems the friends of service rather than its enemies.

UNBLOCKING AND EMPOWERING
MIDDLE MANAGERS

As I have said a number of times in different ways, the key to making the internal service concept work for the organization is to get middle managers out of their "middleman" roles and into leadership roles. They hold in their hands the possibilities for excellence or mediocrity. They exist, whether anybody else likes it or not, and they are the ones who must get turned on to the mission of internal service. This must happen in two ways:

1. Senior management calls upon middle managers to dedicate their departments to service and align their processes with the overall business mission.
2. Middle managers then undertake a systematic redefinition of their departments' roles, contributions, attitudes, and ways of operating.

I hope the discussion in this book so far has provided the motivation and the frame of reference for executives to carry out the first step. The remainder of the book provides a fairly concrete action plan, a set of steps middle managers can go through to put themselves in business as service leaders. I believe we can agree by now that the middle management problem is not a problem in competence or a problem in knowledge or even a problem in commitment. It is a problem in role definition, and we now have the tools, in the context of the internal service approach, to solve that problem.

If the dream comes true, i.e., if a majority of middle managers in the organization take up the flag and place themselves squarely in front of their own individual service revolutions, we have the prospect of an unprecedented degree of organizational focus, alignment, and synergy. This has got to do wonders for the company's competitive capability in its marketplace.

EXECUTIVE COMMITMENT: ARE YOU "FAIR DINKUM"?

Executives in service organizations are rapidly coming to realize how much the success of any service initiative depends on their personal commitment, involvement, and support. There are still some who believe they can simply declare "customer service" to be one of the top five objectives for the year, and everything will turn out fine. There are still some who think they can just sign the check for a customer-service program and buy an improvement in the competitive position.

More and more are realizing that they themselves must *lead* the company through a cultural transformation; it doesn't happen by itself. Consultants can't do it. Task forces can't do it. Highly motivated middle managers can't do it. All of them can contribute to it, but they need the hand of the top person on the throttle to make it really take off.

Not every executive has a charismatic personality and a flair for drama. Not everyone feels comfortable on stage in front of hundreds of employees. Not everyone has "camera presence" or the knack for coming across convincingly on videotape. Each executive has to find his or her own way to express the commitment, genuinely and convincingly. Some chief executives are more cerebral in their approach to their roles. Some are rather homespun. It is important for each one to stay within the realm of what is natural for him or her and believable to the employees.

What really counts is for the chief executive—and the whole top management team—to *be* committed, to act out that commitment, and to show everyone down the line that they will remain committed from now on.

The Australians have an interesting slang term, *fair dinkum*. It means a number of things and probably can't be translated exactly into other forms of English, but essentially it conveys the idea that one is true to his stated beliefs, is determined to live by them, and can be counted on to stay the course. Aussies don't throw the term about lightly. When an Australian executive, usually a male, says, "I intend to show you I'm fair dinkum about this," it's a personal commitment that goes right to the core of being an Aussie. As an American, I wish we had such a useful term in our business culture. But since we don't, I'm sure the Aussies would be happy to loan it to us, so I tend to use it myself. It's such a perfectly descriptive term. So, in Aussie shorthand, the leaders of the company have got to be fair dinkum about it if they expect everybody else to make the commitment. If that happens, it's a fair dinkum company, and it'll be hard to beat.

CHAPTER NOTES

1. Terrence Deal and Allan Kennedy, *Corporate Cultures* (Reading, Mass.: Addison-Wesley, 1984), p. 2.
2. Buck Rogers, *The IBM Way* (New York: Harper & Row, 1986), p. 54.
3. Karl Albrecht, *At America's Service: How Corporations Can Revolutionize the Way They Treat Their Customers* (Homewood, Ill.: Dow Jones–Irwin, 1988), p. 137.
4. Karl Albrecht and Ron Zemke, *Service America!: Doing Business in the New Economy* (Homewood, Ill.: Dow Jones–Irwin, 1985), p. 37.

PART 2

THE PLAN FOR INTERNAL SERVICE

INTRODUCTION TO PART II

THE RECIPE FOR MIDDLE MANAGEMENT LEADERSHIP

If you're a middle manager, you're probably tired of hearing about the middle management problem. You probably don't think of yourself as a problem or an obstacle or a bottleneck. You probably don't consider yourself a bureaucrat (I hope). But if you want to realign your role and that of your department, you're going to do some things they never taught you to do in your management courses.

You're going to have to think strategically and entrepreneurially about your job and about what your department accomplishes. You're going to need a disciplined process, a step-by-step approach to making the kinds of changes that will get your department into the service business if it isn't there already.

Here is a brief overview of the five-stage process presented in the following chapters. If you follow this process faithfully and thoroughly, not short-cutting any of the steps, you can transform your department into a service enterprise that earns its keep.

RECIPE FOR SERVICE LEADERSHIP

1. Get next to your customers and stay there.
2. Define your service mission.
3. Orient your people for service.
4. Focus your systems on service.
5. Focus the rewards on service.

So put on your strategic thinking hat and come with me on a journey that may take you to places you never knew existed. This intellectual journey may be the most important thing you ever do for your department or for the business your department belongs to.

CHAPTER 6

SPECIAL ISSUES FOR INTERNAL SERVICE DEPARTMENTS

ALBRECHT'S LAW: Intelligent people, when assembled
into an organization, can sometimes do dumb things
collectively.

—Karl Albrecht

The following discussion is oriented toward the major complaints and problems people tend to have with various internal service organizations. The portrayals are critical in the sense of presenting the kinds of problems that do occur, with no implication that every or any specific department in a specific organization is guilty of any of them. This is just an attempt to explore the typical perceptions, apparent mind-sets, internal and structural handicaps, and improvement opportunities characteristic of each.

Not all purchasing departments work the same way, but a great many of them are perceived by their customer departments in somewhat the same way. The same is true for data processing departments, personnel departments, and all the rest. Some kinds of service-image problems are so typical that they merit inclusion in a roster of standard pitfalls to avoid.

Your department may not have any of the kinds of image problems described in the following discussion, or it might. In any case, I think they deserve careful consideration from all managers of internal service organizations. For the sake of simplicity, I've reduced the following discussion to a simple catalog-type format, with just a few key factors and comments included for each of the major typical internal service functions one would expect to find in a large organization.

Please read each of these departmental descriptions from the internal customer's point of view, especially when you come to the one for your own department or one similar to it. Be as open-minded as possible.

ACCOUNTING/FINANCE

Somebody once defined accountants and auditors as "the guys who come in after the war's been lost and bayonet the wounded." They are the "money police," the cool, steely-eyed, unemotional keepers of the books. They are the "bean counters" to many operating managers. Many of them deserve that image, and many do not. Nevertheless, people tend to perceive financially oriented departments and functions as exposers and criticizers rather than helpers.

Often Seen as:
- Cold and impersonal.
- Unimaginative; opposed to innovation.
- Not marketing minded.
- Risk-averse.

Typical Customer Complaints:
- "All those guys tell you is what you can't do."
- "They only think about the costs, not the benefits."
- "They can bury you in financial figures, and you don't know what any of it means."

Typical Mind-Set:
- Normative and measurement oriented.
- Passive; uninvolved in business or market strategy.
- Inclined to see other managers as financially ignorant and dangerously irresponsible about costs.
- Respond very cautiously and suspiciously to requests for financial information or planning estimates.

- Tend to see themselves as the keepers of the keys to financial success.

Internal/Structural Handicaps:
- Tend to organize around internal functions; often lack a clear point of contact for their customers to deal with.
- Accuracy orientation sometimes prevents them from thinking hypothetically.
- Sometimes secretive about financial data.

In Their Defense:
- Many managers do not understand the basics of finance very well and do not know how to communicate with finance people.
- Departmental roles are sometimes unclear; sometimes they see themselves as working only for top management.
- Other department heads tend to forget to include finance people in meetings about what's going on; finance people tend to assume it's none of their business.

Can Be More Effective by:
- Helping to educate customer managers in financial thinking.
- Making a greater effort to define the information needs of their customers and communicate with them in terms of those needs.
- Gearing the accounting/finance process and methodology more toward the decision-making needs of executives and managers and less toward the accounting textbook pictures of the organization.

ADMINISTRATIVE SERVICES

Sometimes called the "miscellaneous" department, an administrative service department often has a collection of different types of functions, many of them unrelated to the others. Many of these are "on-call" services, i.e., rendered when people request them, rather than provided on an active ongoing basis. They may include graphics, reproduction, word processing, insurance, medical services, cashier services, facilities repair and maintenance, supplies, and the like.

Often Seen as:
- Uncoordinated and unintegrated; lacking a single point of contact who can help with various matters.
- Hard to get results from; slow-moving and bureaucratic.

Typical Customer Complaints:
- "Try to get a simple thing done, like moving a file cabinet, and they make a five-year project out of it."
- "You can never get a promise from them on when something's going to get done."
- "They act like they're doing you a favor every time you put in a request."

Typical Mind-Set:
- Procedural orientation.
- "If those dumb managers would only follow the proper procedures, we could get things done around here."

Internal/Structural Handicaps:
- Tend to organize according to the types of functions to be performed, which creates a "scattered" customer interface.
- Sometimes feel entitled to set their own priorities for service requests, which sometimes causes a perception of indifference.

In Their Defense:
- Often understaffed.
- Often have so many different functions it's difficult to staff them all effectively.
- Often out of touch with operational planning until somebody drops a request on them.

Can Be More Effective by:

- Setting up single point-of-contact (SPOC) individuals to deal with individual customers to prevent access problems and organizational confusion.
- Explaining to customers how they operate and how the customers can help them do a better job.
- Keeping customers more fully informed about what's going to happen and about status of ongoing projects.

DATA PROCESSING

Data processing departments very commonly have the image of being a bunch of "propeller-heads," i.e., self-absorbed techies who don't deal well with people and who are blissfully indifferent to the pressures of time and the needs of the business.

Often Seen as:

- Preoccupied with technology for its own sake.
- Socially backward; unable to communicate in plain English.
- More concerned with the mechanics of data processing than with the purposes it should serve.
- Unconcerned with and unsympathetic toward the pressing needs of departments who request services; inclined to work at their own speed and offer no sympathy for the manager who must wait many months for results.

Typical Customer Complaints:

- "The place is a black hole. Ask for a simple system change and they tell you it'll be 18 months—if you're lucky."
- "I can't find anybody over there who speaks English."
- "They refuse to listen to what *I* say *I* want; *they* want to tell *me* what I need."

Typical Mind-Set:

- Highly technical, mechanical, thing-oriented world-view; tend to see customers as "users" rather than people with problems and needs.

- "Don't nag me; I'll get to it when I get to it."
- "There's more work than we can handle, so don't worry if you don't get it all done; some of it will probably go away anyway."

Internal/Structural Handicaps:
- Tend to organize along project or project-group lines rather than customer-need lines; constantly changing priorities affect customer timetables, but often are not communicated to the customer.
- Highly technical internal culture makes it difficult for them to think in the customer's terms.
- Sometimes unfamiliar with the basics of the business and cannot appreciate the priorities of operating managers.

In Their Defense:
- Technical training often neglects basic skills of communication and human relations; many technical people are indeed socially handicapped.
- The mission of developing and evolving the total data processing capability often conflicts with the short-term interests and demands of operating managers; they are often in a no-win situation.

Can Be More Effective by:
- Setting up single point-of-contact (SPOC) individuals who can interpret technical information to nontechnical client managers; many data processing departments have done this with the "information center" concept.
- Communicating with customers in plain language instead of technojargon.
- Streamlining access procedures and making their project planning methods more customer-friendly.

FIELD OFFICE

A field office, such as a regional or district headquarters that is supposed to serve a number of commercial operating facilities, i.e., restaurants, hotels, banks, etc., can be a difficult entity to manage from a service standpoint. Not only is the manager of the unit a middle manager, but the whole unit is a middle-of-the-organization unit. It gets pressures from above and below.

Often Seen as:
- Removed from the day-to-day needs and problems.
- Watchdogs and police who do nothing to add value.

Typical Customer Complaints:
- "All they do is kick us in the rear; why don't they help us with our problems?"
- "If they'll just stay out of our hair, that's the most we can hope for."
- "How come we never see these new programs coming until the last minute? They never tell us anything."

Typical Mind-Set:
- Normative view of subsidiary locations as competing against one another.
- "Inspector" attitude; only showing up to conduct an audit or when something is wrong.
- Preoccupation with shortcomings of problem units to the neglect of needs and opportunities of high performers.

Internal/Structural Handicaps:
- Physical distance from the frontline action; hard to understand and appreciate frontline concerns and problems.
- Organizational positioning creates a perception of operating units in simple financial and "production" terms.

In Their Defense:
- Demands from home office often put them in the "middleman" role.
- Often required to push new home-office programs on the field units which may be poorly conceived; must pretend to support them even if they don't understand them.
- Often difficult to overcome field-office suspicion and gain trust to establish a supportive relationship.

Can Be More Effective by:
- Actively seeking feedback from field units about ways to help them.
- Speeding up response mechanisms to get answers and solutions to field units more quickly.

HEADQUARTERS/HOME OFFICE

The "Ivory Tower," the "Puzzle Palace," the "Source of All Knowledge"—the nicknames field people give to the organizational headquarters telegraph clearly how they conceive of the role of that group. Certain perceptions of home office people on the part of field people are very common, regardless of the type of business or organization. Many times they are deserved, and sometimes they are not.

Often Seen as:
- Distant and far removed from the customer and the organizational units that serve the customer.
- Dictatorial and capricious; often issuing directives with no apparent logic or justification.
- An intruder and a time-waster; frequently demanding information and actions for no apparent reason.
- Having little or no appreciation of or concern for the needs and problems of field units.

Typical Customer Complaints:
- "They keep coming out with all these gimmicky programs; they never ask us what *we want* or what *we need*."
- "The only way you can get any help from home office is to know somebody in some department somewhere who will do you a favor."
- "I could spend all my time just filling out these dumb reports and answering these dumb requests for statistics."

Typical Mind-Set:
- Dictatorial attitude toward field units; they must be taught to obey the organizational rules.
- "We know what's best for them; if they'll just put this new program in place and really make it work, everything will be great."
- Tend to see field units as a statistical mass, not as individual operations with individual needs and problems.

Internal/Structural Handicaps:
- Many different departments try to communicate with field units on many unrelated matters; field people get confused and overwhelmed with data, directives, policies, and demands for information.
- Specialized resources reside at headquarters level, creating a temptation to invent everything there and not allow things to originate at field level.

In Their Defense:
- Physical distance does indeed create unavoidable barriers to close relationships with field units.
- Home office role as consolidator and coordinator of the operation is often not understood by field people.
- Field people tend to want levels of autonomy that may not be compatible with a consistent organizational philosophy or customer image which home office must maintain.

Can Be More Effective by:
- Dictating less and listening more.
- Telegraphing new programs and new ventures to the field long before they arrive; giving as much lead time as possible and helping them get ready.
- Actively seeking feedback from field units about ways to support them better.
- Involving selected field people in the development of new programs; including the field perspective in the basic design.

LEGAL

In some organizations, the "legal beagles" are the people to avoid. Their favorite answer seems to be no. They're the people who tell you what you can't do. At any rate, they act like they're always too busy to give you the time of day, so unless you have a real sticky legal problem on your hands, it's better that you don't even mess with them.

Often Seen as:
- The personal lapdogs of senior management, aloof and indifferent toward anybody who doesn't have a lot of organizational clout.
- Much too busy and too important to bother with mundane requests from working-level departments.
- Having virtually no sense of urgency about anything they do.

Typical Customer Complaints:
- "Those guys like to make a mountain out of a molehill. Ask them for a bit of legal advice, and pretty soon they've got you paranoid about all the things that can go wrong."
- "It takes them forever to do anything. You'd like a simple letter of agreement, and after weeks and weeks it comes back a 20-page contract that's bound to scare the pants off the people you're negotiating with."
- "If you're not a vice president or somebody like that, they treat you like you don't exist. They act like they have big, important things to do, and they don't have time to talk to the peasants."

Typical Mind-Set:
- Can be somewhat bureaucratic; tend to think in terms of legal procedures and paperwork rather than in terms of the business problem to be solved.
- Tend to want to cover all possible bases; sometimes create apprehension and the perception of legal problems where none existed before.

- Sometimes have trouble letting go of private-practice habits and techniques in favor of simpler, more streamlined methods appropriate to internal service.

Internal/Structural Handicaps:
- Parkinson's Law often keeps them fully occupied; large, involved projects sometimes interfere with their ability to respond to smaller, ad hoc requests for advice and assistance from departmental customers.
- Many legal people don't recognize units of time smaller than months or, in some cases, weeks; their habit patterns tend to be oriented to the long-term movement of legal documents; this makes it difficult for them to revise their thinking and respond quickly in special cases.

In Their Defense:
- Their advocacy mission puts pressure on them to render safe, prudent opinions; the consequences of committing the organization to a legally untenable course of action can be monstrous; this can lead to a bureaucratic image, even though their caution may be well warranted.
- Many legal questions are indeed complex, and it can be very difficult—and even risky—to dispose of them with quick and dirty legal opinions.
- Many people tend to have biased perceptions of attorneys stemming from their private experiences; these perceptions may contaminate their attitudes toward the legal people in their own organizations.

Can Be More Effective by:
- Making themselves more visible, open, and approachable to their customers.
- Diversifying their "product" to include briefly stated, carefully qualified opinions and legal services that meet special needs, rather than always having to dot the last *i* and cross the last *t*.
- Listening more carefully to the needs and problems of their customers and deciding what level of effort can produce the most useful result under the circumstances.

MANUFACTURING

Manufacturing people often seem to think they have no customers, except the ultimate customer who buys the product. But, in fact, they usually have several other customers. The marketing and salespeople, for example, are often their customers, although not for the physical product. They need information, support, responsive action to correct customer problems, and all the rest. Research and development people, engineering people, and product support people all need things from manufacturing to play their roles effectively.

Often Seen as:
- Process oriented rather than customer or product oriented.
- Set in their ways and resistant to trying new ways of doing things.
- Determined to follow their own procedures and resistant to pleas for streamlining or special actions in unusual situations.

Typical Customer Complaints:
- "Whatever you ask, they tell you it can't be done."
- "They pad their cost estimates so much we can't put together a winning bid."
- "You can't get them to do something quick and dirty for you; they always want to make a million dollars' worth of tooling first."

Typical Mind-Set:
- Everything must be done by procedure; tend to want drawings, specifications, blueprints, etc.; have a hard time with "skunk works" type efforts.
- Tend to see new materials and processes as a disruption to the ways of operating they've learned rather than as ways to make the product more desirable to the customer.

Internal/Structural Handicaps:

- Process orientation often compartmentalizes knowledge and expertise, making it difficult to adapt to new ways of doing things.
- Tendency to organize for large operations makes it difficult to do innovative things for internal customers on a small scale.

In Their Defense:

- Other departments sometimes do not include them in the long-term discussions of product design and technology; sometimes they do not have adequate time to prepare mentally or physically for new approaches.
- Manufacturing departments often operate under severe cost controls, making it difficult for them to find resources to experiment with new methods.
- Research and engineering departments often do design things that can't be built; manufacturing only delivers the bad news, rather than causes it.

Can Be More Effective by:

- Setting up more active liaison activities with technical departments.
- Training key managers to be ambassadors to other departments and importers of new ideas and new trends within the organization.
- Setting up small enclaves that can support the new, unusual, or unorthodox ways of doing things without disrupting the major manufacturing processes.

MARKETING

Marketing people sometimes see themselves as the only force for sanity in the organization. They have a particular view on the world that includes both the outside and the inside. They see the competitive forces outside and the kinds of demands the customer is making, and they see the collective craziness that goes on inside as the organization tries to respond to its environment.

Often Seen as:
- Superficial and Pollyannaish in their thinking.
- Unrealistic about what can be done with technology, products, and pricing.
- Glib talking and somewhat anti-intellectual; lacking in appreciation for the depth of problems and issues.

Typical Customer Complaints:
- "Those guys are always criticizing the product or the price; they just can't make the sale."
- "You can't get them to be specific about customer requirements; it's all handwaving."

Typical Mind-Set:
- Tend to be psychologically disconnected from the day-to-day operation; see themselves as coming in whenever the product is ready and then taking it out to sell it.
- May see price as the primary competitive factor; try to persuade others to allow them to bid lower to get the business; somehow the profit will work itself out.
- Personality type sometimes does not mix well with technical "eggheads" or manufacturing people who are deeply involved in complex specialties.

Internal/Structural Handicaps:
- Selling orientation may prevent them from doing the kind of analytical work needed to develop market information that contributes to good product strategies for other departments.
- Organizational structure may not correspond to communication processes necessary with other departments; for example, organizing by customer type may make it difficult for any one person to speak knowledgeably to technical people who may be organized along product lines.

In Their Defense:
- Other departmental managers sometimes discount the degree of customer knowledge and product awareness that marketing people have.

- Some market/product issues really are as simple as marketing people portray them.

Can Be More Effective by:
- Taking a more active role in educating organizational managers about customer needs and market trends.
- Spending more time with technical and product people, both to learn what they're thinking about for the future and to influence the approaches they take based on customer inputs.

PERSONNEL

Too often, personnel people are out of the mainstream of thinking about the business. Other executives and managers tend to perceive them as taking care of the books of account on human capital and having little to contribute to the strategy and mission of the business. Personnel people often contribute to these perceptions by not speaking up outside of the narrow confines of their recordkeeping mission. Many of them could strengthen the contribution of their departments by taking on more of an advocacy role with respect to human resources effectiveness.

Often Seen as:
- Paper pushers you have to go to to get forms filled out whenever you need to make a personnel change.
- Policy- and procedure-oriented.
- Out of touch with the operational side of the organization.

Typical Customer Complaints:
- "Any time I want to do something out of the ordinary, they throw a policy at me that says I can't do it."
- "I can't find anybody there I can talk to on a confidential basis without having to make a formal personnel action out of it."
- "They don't take direction from me; I want to hire a certain kind of person, but they think they know who I need better than I do."

Typical Mind-Set:

- Normative view of people; tend to prefer numerically based compensation approaches that eliminate ambiguity and judgment with respect to raises and promotions.
- May be legalistically minded with sometimes undue fear of equal-employment problems, lawsuits, etc.; this can interfere with assertive human resource management practices, such as removing ineffective workers and dealing with problem employees.

Internal/Structural Handicaps:

- Sometimes tend to organize along the lines of functional specialties, with the result that a customer manager has no one single point-of-contact (SPOC) for all personnel matters.
- May be so tied to established administrative procedures that they have trouble dealing with unusual personnel problems or issues on an ad hoc basis.

In Their Defense:

- Their advocacy mission includes maintaining a fair and market-oriented compensation system, fair hiring and promotion practices, and control of labor costs; these factors may not be primary in the minds of their customer managers.
- Many customer managers don't like to do their homework prior to trying to recruit new employees; they may tend to expect the personnel department to do their thinking for them.

Can Be More Effective by:

- Establishing SPOC-type structures to help managers gain easy access to all personnel functions without having to navigate the organization chart.
- Helping educate customer managers in effective recruitment, hiring, and placement practices.
- Adopting a practical view of human resources effectiveness that enables them to help managers remove ineffec-

tive employees, develop those who have the potential, and deal quickly with those who should not be in the organization.

- Adopting a more aggressive role with respect to the development of management expertise at all levels and the use of effective management practices.

PUBLIC RELATIONS

The "PR" people are often some of the least understood and least relied-on people in the organization. Most PR groups could be much more effective by getting more involved in the operation of the business and staying in closer touch with managers who need to communicate messages to the various publics whose perceptions are important to the success of the organization.

Often Seen as:
- Superficial, jolly folk who want everybody to be happy.
- Paid corporate liars whose job is to create fiction and sell it to the public.
- People who try to manufacture news out of little or nothing of substance.

Typical Customer Complaints:
- "I can't get them to sit down and listen to me long enough to understand the real issues we're trying to communicate.
- "They can't tell the difference between truth and falsehood; they say things that aren't really true or that we can't back up."
- "They make their own news; we could supply them with lots of newsworthy items, but they never ask."

Typical Mind-Set:
- Tend to avoid complex or potentially controversial news issues; prefer the bland, "image" type of topics.
- Sometimes intimidated by journalists; often don't have clear objectives in approaching a PR opportunity.

- Tend to assume they know what's best for the image; often do not understand the strategic positioning of the company and its needs to communicate to the business environment.

Internal/Structural Handicaps:
- Sometimes tend to be media oriented rather than issues oriented; this may cause them to favor topics and methods of presentation that favor communication media they feel comfortable with.
- Often do not have reliable news-gathering mechanisms; tend to accept whatever comes along and try to work with it.

In Their Defense:
- Most customer managers tend not to think in PR terms; not inclined to include PR people in their thinking and planning.
- As generalists, they often don't have the background to understand and interpret complex business or technical issues; must rely on managers for interpretations.
- Journalists tend to have very definite ideas about how they want to present the news; often resist influence from sources with respect to slant and coverage; PR people sometimes have limited opportunities to present a case.

Can Be More Effective by:
- Maintaining close personal relationships with the thought leaders of the organization.
- Gaining greater depth of knowledge about current business and technical issues within the organization.
- Teaching customer managers how to recognize PR implications of what's going on.

PURCHASING

Some purchasing people have earned the image of the ultimate bureaucrat: whatever you think you want to do, they know better. Some of them take it upon themselves to decide what's really important, and the managers who are trying to acquire goods and services will have to "like it or lump it."

Often Seen as:
- Bureaucratic, procedurally minded, and utterly unconcerned with the time pressures faced by their customers.
- Tending to second-guess the customer manager who has an idea about how he or she wants to approach a particular procurement action.
- Overly committed to paperwork, contracts, specifications, and procurement procedures, often at the expense of timeliness and sometimes out of proportion to the magnitude of the matter at hand.

Typical Customer Complaints:
- "It takes forever to get them to do anything. By the time they assign a purchasing agent and that person gets all the paperwork together and gets ready to move, the project is over with."
- "They don't want to do things in the simplest way. They have to go to three competing vendors just to buy a nut and a bolt."
- "I told them there's only one vendor in the country who makes this particular machine, but they insist that I write up a detailed specification so they can shop it around; they'll end up buying it from this vendor anyway, but the whole process will take months."

Typical Mind-Set:
- Inclined to feel that customer managers are basically lazy and don't want to exert the necessary effort to get the best prices and best terms from suppliers.
- Sometimes can't distinguish between large, high-consequence matters and small, low-consequence matters; tend to want to use the same formal procedures for both.
- Tend to have little patience with rush projects, feeling managers should have planned more carefully to allow procurement lead time.

Internal/Structural Handicaps:

- Tend to organize for a transactional mode of doing business, i.e., see themselves as "processing purchase orders" rather than helping customer departments acquire goods and services they need to meet their objectives.
- Relate to customer departments on an "input-output" basis rather than a cooperative problem solving basis: i.e., the operational mode is "give me a purchase request and I'll take it from there," rather than "let's sit down and figure out how to get what you need quickly and cost-effectively."

In Their Defense:

- Purchasing people have an advocacy mission of assuring that the organization gets value for its money; they have techniques that can save cost and get good deals from suppliers, and it's their job to advocate good procurement practices.
- Many customer managers do not allow enough planning time for procurement and sometimes expect the purchasing department to cut corners in order to meet their schedules.

Can Be More Effective by:

- Forming closer working relationships with customer managers, so they can see major problems coming sooner.
- Helping to educate managers about purchasing approaches that can get better value for money.
- Being more willing to use streamlined methods when the urgency of the situation calls for it.

RESEARCH AND DEVELOPMENT

"The eggheads," "the wizards," "malfunction junction"—these are some of the terms people in other departments use to refer to people in engineering, research, and development areas. Dealing as they do with highly technical matters all day long, sometimes they do find it difficult to communicate clearly with ordinary earthlings.

Often Seen as:

- Cerebral, somewhat other-worldly, and often not very practical or commonsensical.
- Engrossed in exotic technical issues that may not relate to the practical needs of the business.
- Difficult to communicate with, inarticulate, socially backward, and having little patience with people who don't understand the subjects they're talking about.

Typical Customer Complaints:

- "Asking one of those guys a simple question is like taking a drink from a fire hose; ask him what time it is and he'll start telling you how to make a watch."
- "They can never stop playing with something and put it into production; they keep trying to perfect it until the cows come home."
- "It's hard to get a rough-cut answer from them; you may just want a quick and dirty technical opinion on something, but they refuse to commit themselves without a detailed technical analysis."

Typical Mind-Set:

- Enjoy dealing with complex technical issues for their own sake; get pleasure out of grappling with difficult issues, sometimes whether they have practical value or not.
- Take great pride in solving problems effectively; dislike having to give quick answers without having thought carefully about a technical question.
- Tend to have little tolerance for nontechnical people who try to delve into technical matters, especially those who don't accept their opinions on face value.

Internal/Structural Handicaps:

- Tend to organize along the lines of technical specialty; often make it difficult for people in other departments to know whom to contact when they need information.

- Tend to be introverted, socially retiring people with limited human relations skills; often dislike having to deal with people, especially those outside their own realm.

In Their Defense:
- Some issues or problems require a fair degree of technical knowledge to interpret and resolve; nontechnical people sometimes have little patience with the complexity involved and may insist on simple answers.
- Nontechnical people often cannot reliably estimate the amount of effort, time, and cost involved in solving some of the problems they pose; they may place very unrealistic expectations on technical people, assuming they can produce breakthroughs on demand.

Can Be More Effective by:
- Learning more effective interpersonal and communications skills.
- Taking more time to explain technical matters to those who need to understand them in order to support their proposed courses of action.
- Compromising sometimes with the needs and purposes of others; being somewhat less technically "pure" for the sake of practical solutions.

TRAINING/HUMAN RESOURCE DEVELOPMENT

Most training departments do not earn anywhere near the degree of influence they should have, nor are they as effective in delivering their product as they could be. Most managers in other parts of the organization typically view them as harmless, friendly folks, but not as people essential to accomplishing the business mission. Many people see "going to a training program" as a form of recreation, a relief from the normal day's work routine, rather than an important experience in making them more able to accomplish their missions.

Often Seen as:
- The company "schoolhouse"; the place you go when your boss decides you need to take a course.
- Off in the corner; uninvolved in the problems of the organization.
- A discretionary item on the budget; funded at a modest level; one of the first items to be cut when the budget gets tight and one of the last to be restored when things get better.

Typical Customer Complaints:
- "They never seem to have any programs that relate to the needs of my department."
- "If I ask them for something that's not in their catalog, they tell me to do it myself."
- "Their programs are all generic; they don't focus on the problems and needs of this organization."

Typical Mind-Set:
- Passive, uninvolved in the real problems of the organization; waiting for someone to invite them to the game.
- Feel unappreciated and unrecognized for the contribution they can make; "They won't use our services; we always have to push them into sending people to training."
- Tend to be oriented to process more than outcome, i.e., often think in terms of classroom training rather than in terms of problems to be solved and competencies to be developed in key people.

Internal/Structural Handicaps:
- Often set up to operate the company schoolhouse, rather than to work actively with managers to help them develop their staff capabilities.
- Tend to favor modes of education they feel comfortable with, typically classroom presentation; often not set up to exploit the possibilities of alternative methods such as closed-circuit video, teleconferencing, university extension programs, public seminars, and specialized conferences.

- Often do not take a broad enough view of the educational mission; fail to recognize the difference between outcomes and means for achieving them.

In Their Defense:

- Senior executives often do not recognize the potential of employee education and often do not support it or invest in it adequately.
- Customer managers often do not recognize their own responsibilities for employee development; they tend to assume the training department takes care of training and often do not understand that they are ultimately responsible for the training, education, and career development of all employees in their units.

Can Be More Effective by:

- Knowing a lot about the organization's customers, products, operations, problems, issues, and strategies, so they can talk knowledgeably with customer managers about their needs and objectives.
- Staying in close touch with customer managers and coaching them toward a much more proactive approach to developing their own staffs.
- Being willing to develop special training solutions to meet very specific organizational challenges.
- Gaining access to the thoughts, feelings, and worries of senior executives and showing them how employee development can play a part in achieving the organizational mission.

CHAPTER 7

UNDERSTANDING THE INTERNAL CUSTOMER

I kept six honest serving men;
They taught me all I knew.
Their names were What, and Why, and When,
And How, and Where, and Who.
> —*Rudyard Kipling*

FIGURING OUT WHO THE CUSTOMERS ARE

It may sound peculiar, but the first step in committing your organization to serving its customers effectively is to find out who they are. Internal service organizations often have more complicated roles and relationships than those that work directly with the paying customer. Some departments know very clearly and simply who their customers are, while others are not so sure.

Some departments have clear customer relationships with some customers and not-so-clear relationships with others. It's no disgrace to be a bit vague about your customers; it may only mean that your department has one of those roles that affect various people indirectly.

In speeches to managers I often say, only partly in jest, "If you don't know who your customers are, there's a simple test you can perform to find out. Just stop doing whatever you're doing for two weeks and see who starts to complain. That's your customer. If nobody complains, you'd better flip the switch on your word processor and update your resume."

✳— Actually, this is not a bad way to do it, at least in your mind. Start by asking yourself, "Who would be inconvenienced, and how, if my department stopped operating?" "What departments or people would have trouble accomplishing their mission without the results of what we do?" "Who would be affected directly and who indirectly?" Start writing some notes as you think this through.

Here's a horrifying thought: allow for the possibility that they really don't need you. What would you do if you really came to the honest conclusion that your group served no useful purpose or that your activities so overlapped those of other groups—including your supposed customers—that the organization could get along without it? Would you have the courage to say so? Well, let's assume for this discussion that you do have valid reasons for existing, and they just need clarifying. Begin itemizing some of the categories of people, units, or interest groups in the organization who need your contribution to their effectiveness. Avoid the temptation to say, "Everybody is my customer. I serve the whole organization." That's too diffuse an answer. You need to zero in on your *primary* customer—the one who needs you most. First decide on that, and later on you can extend your thinking to others.

Perhaps you can identify your primary customer immediately. Your function may be so clear and well defined that you have only one customer. In that case, the next few paragraphs probably won't apply to you. But please review them just in case they say anything that might lead you to rethink the relationship, even slightly.

But let's suppose you draw a blank at first. Suppose you know what you do, but you don't do it for people on a one-to-one or face-to-face basis. The next step, in that case, is to apply the service management thinking and look for the moments of truth. Remember that a moment of truth is any episode in which your customer comes into contact with any aspect of your organization and gets an impression of your service.

How does the customer, or anyone for that matter, experience the results of what you do? Does someone receive a report? Turn on a piece of equipment and need to have it operate properly? Look up information in a computer that you've put there?

Walk into a lobby or reception area or work space and find it clean and attractively maintained? Read certain financial figures and feel pleased? These people are some of your customers. You need to continue this kind of itemization until you feel confident you have identified your interface with the rest of the organization.

Once you have a good start on identifying your customers, see if you can *segment* them somehow, according to the kinds of interests they have in your service. For example, you might segment users of a data processing capability in terms of the clerical people who work at the keyboards, the supervisors who need current information to do department jobs, and higher level managers who need various special services to support their unit missions. These three customer groups will have distinctly different views of the service, and each will have a unique set of needs.

Assuming you have identified your customers, at least categorically, and segmented them into logical groups based on their various service needs, it's time to work on understanding them as customers. Start making notes on your own at first, and later visit with some of them to learn how they look at your service. Ask yourself questions like, "How does our service affect their operations?" "What special problems do they have that we need to understand?" "When we fail to do our jobs well, what are the adverse effects on them?" and "Which of their needs are the most critical?"

Draw up a specific profile for each of your major customers or types of customers. For each one, write down whether they experience your service directly or indirectly. Write down a description of the way they experience it: i.e., how does the interface with that particular customer work? This will give you a basic start. During this customer identification process, feel free to contact various people you think are customers, might be customers, or should be customers. Find out how aware they are of your service, what they think you do, and the impressions they have of the contribution you are supposed to make.

Put all of this information together into a simple written statement that describes the constituency you believe your organization should be serving, with some general indication of the nature of the service you believe they need. Then you're ready to get some feedback from them.

GETTING CUSTOMER FEEDBACK

The easiest way to get customer feedback is just to ask for it in a straightforward, innocent way. Make appointments with key customers or with certain people who exemplify the types of customers you're dealing with and sit down with them for a discussion. Tell them what you're trying to accomplish and ask them to help you understand your service as they perceive it.

This process doesn't have to be terribly scientific at first. It's important to listen carefully and nondefensively and to allow yourself an opportunity to discover aspects of your service, as perceived by the customer, which you may not have considered in the past. Ask them to give it to you, warts and all. Be especially careful not to try to rebut anything they say, counterattack, or trade accusations. That will only shut off the flow of information. Leave your ego back at your office and just gather information.

Your objective in this feedback-gathering process is to find out how your customers conceive of the service they expect from you and how they perceive it as they actually get it. If there are differences, you certainly want to discover them.

You might want to use a combination of one-on-one interviews with selected customers and small-group discussions, almost like focus groups. Some people will be more candid in private, others in a group situation.

Don't make any overly ambitious attempts to measure the quality of your service at this point. You'll probably overwhelm your customers with questionnaires and score sheets before you've really defined the quality variables you need to measure. At this point, seek a qualitative understanding of their needs and a general sense of how they see the service they're getting.

CONDUCTING A SERVICE AUDIT

At this point, consider conducting a general *service audit* to get a concrete sense of what your customers are experiencing. A service audit is a sampling of selected aspects of the customer interface to get an idea how well it operates overall and to highlight any problematical aspects of the service package you provide. Just as a general audit by an accountant doesn't delve into every detail of the business, but evaluates certain key features of the financial practices to make sure they're properly carried out, so a service audit looks for key signs of service performance.

A service audit might investigate several different types of service or several different aspects of the service. It might include, for example, a step-by-step review of a selected cycle of service to see how well it works. It might also include in-depth interviews with one or more representative customers to see how they feel about their experiences. It might include discussions with typical service employees to see how they feel about the service product. This process can easily overlap to some extent with the process of gathering customer feedback just previously described.

The main objective of the service audit is to identify priorities for further investigation and possible areas for immediate improvement. It can also help you form a clearer picture of the service relationship you want to establish with your customers and help you get ready for the thinking process required to define your service mission.

IDENTIFYING AND ANALYZING YOUR
MOMENTS OF TRUTH

The entire foundation of service management rests on the concept of *moments of truth* as the basic defining elements of service—the fundamental "atoms" that make up the product. To apply service management thinking, you must start by identifying your moments of truth with the customer. Earlier we saw that looking for moments of truth could be a helpful way to begin clearing up the question of who the customer is. Now you are ready to conduct a thorough, disciplined review of every type of moment of truth you can find.

You will probably find many, perhaps hundreds of different moments of truth involved in delivering your service product. Here are some typical types of moments of truth, to get your thinking started.

1. Customer calls your department.
2. Contact person answers a request.
3. Customer receives information from your department.
4. Service person visits the customer's area.
5. Customer complains to someone about the quality of the service.
6. Customer uses a piece of equipment you provide.
7. Customer requests additional information.
8. Customer receives a charge for your services.
9. Customer asks for an unusual procedure or service.
10. Customer fills out a form you provide.

Note how each moment of truth involves the customer directly and focuses on the way the customer experiences the situation. Consider moment of truth number 10 above, for example. Have you ever thought of filling out a form as a moment of truth? Can you remember having to wrestle with a complex, confusing form that demanded information in all sorts of inconvenient formats, forced you to do tedious calculations, or forced you to look up hard-to-find data? Think about how you felt. Friendly forms are one of the most effective improvements we can make in virtually all service businesses, both internal and external.

Sit down with the key members of your team and go through a brainstorming session. Without getting sidetracked by details or discussion of particulars, just start rattling off moments of truth and writing them down on a list. Remember that a moment of truth is something the customer sees, so don't mix backroom processes in with this list; we'll analyze those later. Don't worry about organizing any of the information at this point; just get it down on paper. Challenge the group's thinking in every way possible to pinpoint even the most obscure or occasional moments of truth.

Don't be satisfied with this process until you can look at the list and say to yourself, "Yes, this is our customer interface." Leaving out any important moments of truth at this stage will only weaken your analysis later on. Pry into every nook and cranny of your activities, looking for undiscovered points of customer impact. Then step back and ask yourself whether you've overlooked any that are so obvious that they don't even come to mind. The better the job you do at this point, the stronger your quality model will be later on.

At this point, it's probably a good idea to have the moments of truth organized and typed into a readable and workable list. Give a copy to each of your key people and allow time for everyone to review it and think about it. Now you're ready to begin analyzing the various moments of truth.

Start by grouping the moments of truth into logical categories, if appropriate. Do some of them affect only certain kinds of customers? Do some involve personal contact and others involve impersonal impacts on the customer? Are some of them individualized, while others affect people all at once?

Next, identify the *critical moments of truth* on your list. A critical moment of truth is one that has unusually important implications for customer satisfaction. If things go wrong here, there can be serious problems with the customer. You might find that only 5 to 10 percent of the moments of truth on your list are extremely critical, while the rest contribute about equally to satisfaction. You must have an approach for managing all moments of truth effectively, but you need to single out the critical moments of truth for special attention.

Now, for both the critical moments of truth and the regular ones, begin to associate various quality criteria with each. What counts at this particular moment of truth? Timeliness? Accuracy of information? Current, up-to-date information? Friendly personal treatment? Response time? Ease of use of equipment? The general appearance of a facility? The cost of something? You may find many different quality criteria, and you will probably begin to find that a few of them seem most important in most cases.

Bear in mind at this point that these are only your own perceptions of the quality factors involved in the moments of truth. Later on, you will have an opportunity to validate your estimates by getting more feedback from your customers.

Finish this part of the analysis by cleaning up and refining the list of moments of truth, categorize them as you see fit, flag the critical ones, and make copies of the list for all of your key people to study and think about.

IDENTIFYING AND ANALYZING YOUR CYCLES OF SERVICE

The *cycle of service* model is one of the most important tools of service management because it enables you to diagram and analyze the service *as your customer sees it*. Most systems-analysis diagraming methods focus on the organizational mechanisms, with only an afterthought given to the customer's point of view. The cycle of service forces you to deal with those elements of the customer's experience that lead him or her to form an impression of the quality of your service.

Cycles of service are going on all over the organization all the time. Here are some examples of typical cycles of internal service, as seen from the point of view of the person in the organization who wants to accomplish something:

1. Hiring a new employee.
2. Purchasing a piece of equipment.
3. Getting a legal opinion on a course of action.
4. Having a software program written.
5. Having one's office moved.
6. Shipping a package to another country.
7. Getting an advance on travel funds.
8. Having a special accounting report prepared.
9. Sending an employee to a training seminar.
10. Having briefing aids prepared for a meeting.

Think about each of these cycles, first as the person trying to get something done, and second as the head of the department responsible for providing the service. Can you sense an immediate difference in the two points of view? The customer may do this thing very seldom, while the service department does it for a living. The service department will have worked out a system for doing it, but will the system be friendly to the customer's needs? You start analyzing the cycles of service in much the same way as you started with the individual moments of truth—by finding out what they are. Begin to think through your line of services and itemize the various kinds of actions the customer takes to get his or her needs met through your operation. Note that the cycle of service usually starts with something the customer does, although not always. It has a logical beginning, a series of steps, and a conclusion. Note that the cycle is only complete when the customer considers it complete, not just when you believe you're finished.

A certain amount of practice in drawing cycles of service for various operations will give you a bit of skill with it. Here are some things to think about in diagraming service cycles. First, decide how detailed you want to make the diagram. You can get too microscopic sometimes by including every arm and head movement the customer makes. Just pick a reasonable level of detail that will enable you to deal with the major events in the cycle. Conversely, don't make it too macroscopic, or you won't be getting to the key factors that affect quality.

Second, recognize that some cycles of service are much more complex than others. They may involve variations you can't necessarily represent all on one diagram. Some cycles may involve loops, in which a certain process repeats a number of times before the rest of the cycle proceeds. There may be cycles within cycles, so to speak. Your goal in analyzing cycles of service is not to account for every little thing that goes on, but rather to understand the interaction with the customer well enough to know what makes for quality. You also want to spot portions of the cycle that invite improvement.

Some cycles of service may be so simple as to seem trivial. Some may only have two or three moments of truth, even though the supporting processes may be rather complicated. In such a case, bear in mind that these few moments of truth the customer experiences are all you have to create a perception of service quality.

When a service provider feels the customer doesn't appreciate the value received, it may be because the customer interface is somewhat "impoverished," i.e., gives too little evidence to the customer of the service being performed behind the scenes. In such cases, it might make sense to look for ways to enrich the interface. This doesn't mean pestering the customer just to create more moments of truth, but rather adding value to the service product and at the same time helping the customer experience the value of the service more fully.

Here are some things to begin thinking about with respect to the quality of service experienced by the customer through these cycles:

1. *Complexity:* The more complex the cycle, the lower the probability the customer will be happy with the whole thing. Frankly, each moment of truth is an opportunity to drop the ball, and the more moments of truth you have, the more times it can happen.

2. *Number of players:* The more people involved in the cycle, the lower the probability of satisfaction. People have to communicate to work together, and more people mean more possibilities for misunderstandings, misstatements, wrong information passed along, and incorrect assumptions about the customer's need. Someone can forget to tell something to someone else, and the whole cycle can go wrong.

3. *Handoffs:* The more handoffs, i.e., transfers between departments, the lower the probability of satisfaction. Different work groups have different perspectives on the service and different habits of operating. Interactions between groups mean possibilities for errors and omissions. If the form doesn't go from department A to department B, department C is going to be in trouble with the customer.

4. *Demands on the customer:* The more knowledge, investigation, decision making, and follow-through required of the customer, the higher the probability something will go wrong. Too many service organizations force the customer to do a research job to get his or her needs met. Somebody should be managing the customer's experience through the cycle. In many cases the organization forces the customer to manage the interface instead of managing it for him.

This is not to paint an unreasonably pessimistic picture of the customer interface, but just to make the point that excellent service doesn't happen by chance. Keep in mind that:

When the moments of truth go unmanaged, quality of service regresses to mediocrity.

This points up the crucial importance of understanding the cycles of service, designing them to be as foolproof as possible, and managing them in day-to-day operation.

A reasonable approach to identifying and analyzing your cycles of service is to make a list of the major ones, diagram each one, look for the critical moments of truth in each one, evaluate each one in terms of its potential for failure and opportunities for improvement, and write each one up for discussion. Then get together with your key people, and begin to study the major cycles, one by one. Then you are ready to get a better idea of how the customer defines quality in these cycles of service and what factors you want to be able to manage in order to make sure they all deliver a quality service product.

DEVELOPING A CUSTOMER REPORT CARD

To manage a service operation effectively, you need a quality model that tells you what good service is. We have been heading in that direction with the analysis of moments of truth and cycles of service. Now you're ready to extract the quality criteria you will use to measure how well you do and correct problem areas when necessary. You need to put together a "customer report card."

A customer report card is a framework for scoring the service you provide, according to criteria you have validated as being important to your customers. If you've been progressing in the analysis described above, you've certainly been getting impressions about the factors your customers consider important. And, of course, you've known about many of these factors from previous experience. Now you're ready to put them together into your best estimate of the "grading system" that makes sense for your service product.

Your departmental report card will be unique to your operation. The factors you include will depend on how you view your relationship to your customers. If you serve several very different kinds of customers or perform very different kinds of services, it might be necessary to work out more than one report card, perhaps one for each major variation.

Here is the general method for compiling your customer report card. First, look at the list of moments of truth and the list of cycles of service, and begin making a list of potential *service attributes.* There are the scoring factors you want to consider. A service attribute is a characteristic of the service product, as perceived by the customer, which has value for the customer. It is a feature of the customer interface that he or she appreciates.

Examples of service attributes could be:

1. Friendliness of your direct-contact people.
2. Speed in getting things to your customer.
3. Quality of information you provide, i.e., accuracy, timeliness.
4. Technical expertise of your people who consult with the customer.
5. Reliability and availability of equipment you provide.
6. Administrative convenience in dealing with your department.
7. Lead times for accomplishing major activities.
8. Ready availability of someone who can give quick answers.
9. Flexibility in responding to unusual requests.
10. Ability to communicate in nontechnical language.

Your service attributes may or may not be on this list. The key is to identify all the factors you believe represent quality and value to your customers. The next step is to validate the criteria on your list by talking to the customers.

Schedule interviews with key customers, and ask them to help you evaluate the various quality factors you have identified so far. Ask them if they can think of any other important criteria that affect the quality of your service product. During the discussions, gather information about the relative desirability of the factors as well. Which ones do the customers really cherish? Which ones are merely nice to have? You may find that two or three factors top the list and that the others come along fairly far behind. You may start with 15 or 20 factors and find that only 7 of them really count. The others may play a part, but the idea is to isolate the really crucial quality criteria.

Once you have a short list of quality factors you really trust, you have the basis of your customer report card. A later chapter explains how to set up a service quality measurement system based on this report card.

MEASURING INTERNAL SERVICE QUALITY

You and your people need *feedback* if you want to keep the quality of your service high. You need objective information that tells you how your customers feel about your service and where they feel you need to improve. You need a Service Quality Measurement System or SQMS.

A service quality measurement system consists of at least the following parts:

1. A quality model, which is your customer report card.
2. A system for gathering feedback data about the quality factors.
3. A method for analyzing the feedback data.
4. A regular reporting system that presents the results.

Let's examine these parts one at a time. We've already mentioned the customer report card, which is a validated set of quality attributes, or criteria for scoring the critical aspects of your customer interface. The following discussion assumes you have your customer report card fully developed and ready for use as a measurement tool.

Next, you need to set up some method for gathering the feedback data. You can do this in at least three ways. For one, you can simply call on—or have a staff person call on—selected customers who will frequently be managers and ask them to respond to a series of questions based on the service quality factors. This can be either a telephone survey or a face-to-face visit. You must be considerate of the customers' time, so they don't begin to feel you're pestering them and taking more of their time than the situation calls for. But it is important to get current readings from them on the various quality factors.

The second thing you can do is create a survey questionnaire that asks for ratings on each of the key quality factors. You can send this to your customers periodically and ask them to fill it out and send it back to you. This will give you a broader statistical picture of peoples' reactions and can possibly eliminate certain biases that might exist in face-to-face interviewing.

And the third approach you can use is "spot" quality surveys at the actual level of the service you perform. Just as restaurants and hotels give their customers feedback cards to evaluate individual dining experiences or hospitality experiences, you can ask your customers to evaluate specific service episodes. You could very easily develop a simple question card with just a few key items that would give you a very current, tactical picture of service quality as seen by your customers at the point of contact. You might choose to make these spot surveys somewhat more specific than the overall customer report card.

Again, remember with all of these approaches that your customers won't want to be bombarded with feedback instruments every day. There will be a limit to their willingness to respond, so use them strategically. Remember that your internal customers are virtually all repeat customers because they deal with you every time they need your type of service. They're not like hotel customers, who pass by in large numbers and partake of your services once or a few times at most. So they may easily get tired of hearing from you. You needn't be offended by this reaction, but it is important to deal with it constructively.

I recall working with a hospital in which we developed a feedback card aimed at getting physicians to evaluate the hospital's service to them every time they admitted a patient for a stay. Some of them were happy to return the cards after every admission, while others said, in effect, "Look, I've told you on various cards about the problems I thought needed fixing.

You've looked after those problems, and I'm well satisfied with everything. Don't send me any more of these cards. I'll let you know when I'm really concerned about something." Even in those cases we sent them an occasional survey card, but we honored their preferences to be left alone.

Once you have your data-gathering method set up, you next have to work out a method for analyzing the data conveniently and efficiently. If you're sufficiently serious about measuring your service quality, you'll want to make this a regular, routine monitoring process, not a once-a-year episode.

Consider appointing someone to gather and organize the incoming feedback sheets, keep track of them by date or month, and analyze the results numerically. If you have access to a personal computer system, consider using a statistical software package that can help you process survey results. One such package, designed for statistical novices, is "Custometrics," published by Shamrock Press (Division of Karl Albrecht & Associates) in San Diego.[1]

Let's say you have chosen to keep up a statistical quality monitoring system based on your customer report card. In that case, you need to develop a simple report format that lends itself to quick interpretation of the feedback results. If your customer report card has seven factors on it, your service quality report should have these same seven factors, with statistical scores for each.

Consider using the basic five-point multiple choice rating scale, which many people find easy to use and which you will find easy to read on the report. Use a scale with 1 meaning a low score and 5 meaning a high score. This way, when you and your key people look at the reports, you can tell at a glance which factors got the best scores. Follow the traditional pattern: big number means good score.

Your SQMS can give you regular information on the vital signs of your operation as seen by your customers. Once you have this flow of information, it's important to act upon it. Give the service quality report to your subordinate managers and your key employees. Feel free to give it to all staff members, and make sure they understand the story it tells. Use the feedback to recruit everyone to the cause of responsive, quality service.

Help everyone in your organization become more customer minded and quality minded. Integrate the SQMS information into your operation just as you would any other important business information.

CHAPTER NOTES

1. *Custometrics: The Customer Satisfaction Survey System,* Shamrock Press, Division of Karl Albrecht & Associates, 1277 Garnet Avenue, San Diego, California 92109, USA. (619) 272-3880.

CHAPTER 8

DEFINING THE INTERNAL SERVICE MISSION

Fanatic: a person who redoubles his efforts when he's lost sight of his aim.

—Anonymous

Once you've done all the essential things under the first step, as described in the previous chapter, you are in a position to define your *service mission.* Why do you need a service mission? Because you need to be able to explain to yourself, your key people, your employees, and your customers why your department exists. A mission statement answers the question, "Why does the organization need us?" Developing your mission statement can be a very challenging thing, depending on the nature of your department's involvement in the organization. It can also be a very enlightening experience because it can lead you to a much clearer understanding of what's important about what you do.

The first thing you have to do in order to move toward a worthwhile mission statement is figure out what business you're in.

WHAT IS YOUR ORGANIZATION'S BUSINESS (*NOT* YOUR BUSINESS ACTIVITY)?

One of the concepts that made Peter F. Drucker famous as the leading thinker in western management is his favorite question: "What business are you in?" According to Drucker, many chief executives can't answer the question clearly and simply, even though it's a simple question. Because they can't answer it clearly, they have trouble in their own minds with setting direction and choosing priorities. They tend to drift and grope, trying to get their organizations to do a little bit of everything.

According to Drucker, a company must focus its efforts carefully if it is to survive and prosper. Too many organizations scatter their energies because of lack of focus. This essential focus of energy requires a clear direction and a clear determination of what the company has to do in its market to succeed. Just as the service business needs a clear understanding of what business it is in, so a service-oriented internal department needs to answer the same question for its activities. What business are *you* in?

There is an almost universal tendency among middle managers to preoccupy themselves with the *activities* their departments carry out and to have a great deal of difficulty thinking on the level of mission. If you ask the head of a teller-training group in a bank, "What is your business?" you will probably get an answer like "We train tellers." Ask the head of the transportation department in a hospital the question, and he or she will probably say, "We move patients from one department to another." The head of an accounts payable unit in the accounting division may say, "We process vendor invoices for payment."

In all of these examples, you didn't get an answer to the question, "What is your business?" What you got was a statement of the department's *business activity* and the *business concept.* You have to think at the level of the business concept first, in order to get a clear idea what the business activity should be. There are many internal service departments in many companies doing things nobody needs to have done. Carried along on their own bureaucratic inertia, they operate on an activity-based concept of what they do, not a mission-based concept.

Your job as a service leader is to determine what your department's business really is, i.e., the ultimate value or benefit your activities can bring about for the good of the organization. This *organizing principle*, this statement of value, becomes the foundation for a rational thought process that gives meaning to the question of what your people do every day.

FORGET FUNCTIONS—THINK ABOUT CONTRIBUTIONS

The starting point for figuring out what business you're in is the *contribution* your department can make to the overall success of the organization. Forget about the *"functions"* you supposedly perform: auditing, transportation, mail delivery, X-raying, purchasing, personnel, training, financial analysis, field support, and all the rest. Think about *contributions*; think about *outcomes*. What is the supposed result of what you do? What are you trying to make happen in the organization? What state of affairs would give evidence of worthwhile effort on the part of your department?

If you know clearly the contribution you want your department to make to the organization, you will find it much easier to define, shape, plan, and set objectives for the activities that should go on.

How do you express your contribution? This is a creative mental act for which no formula or recipe exists. You can't choose it from a list of standard contributions. But you can search your mind for words or concepts that capture the essence of the value you intend to deliver. Think of your contribution in terms of an outcome—a result or a state of affairs you intend to bring about or maintain. Maybe some examples will help your thinking.

In a discussion with the head of an employee development department in a major hospital, she said at first, "My contribution is training programs." I objected gently, saying, "I think a training program is one way of *making* a contribution. What's the contribution itself? What is the outcome of the training program?" Her response was, "Well, I guess the outcome is competent people." That struck me as a much better statement of contribution, and she felt she could take action based on it. If the contribution is competent people, not training programs, she is free to consider a broad range of activities that can contribute to the result of competent people. Counseling, work-study programs, university extension programs, professional conferences, certification programs—all can play a part in developing competence among the organization's people. Another interesting example, again from the hospital business, involved a department called "utilization management." The utilization management people have the responsibility of monitoring the rates at which physicians utilize various expensive hospital services such as X ray, blood tests, CAT scans, arthroscopy, and the like, in treating patients covered by standard-payment health maintenance programs.

The hospital gets paid by these sources on a flat-rate basis according to the illness, not a direct-billing basis according to the services used. The hospital has to keep the utilization of services within bounds so it can cover the costs of the treatment and make a surplus from the payments.

The head of utilization management was having trouble figuring out who her customers were and how to express her contribution. After a discussion she decided that the doctors were her customers because she had to keep them happy while reminding them about the utilization guidelines. The service departments were also her customers because her activities affected their planning and resource levels. And she saw the top management team as her customer because they needed information on utilization rates across the various specialties.

When she attacked the question of her contribution, she decided the outcome she wanted was a certain pattern of *practice profiles*, i.e., rates of utilization that were appropriate for the various specialties involved. So she decided to express her contribution in terms of achieving and maintaining appropriate practice profiles through a combination of feedback and gentle persuasion.

Prior to this, she had described her activities in terms of measuring practice profiles, preparing reports, conferring with doctors, and meeting with senior management to resolve utilization problems. Now she had a clearer sense of her contribution, and she began to conceive of other aspects of her customer relationships based on this new angle of approach.

Perhaps a third example will provide enough food for

thought; then you can take it from there. The head of data processing in a large utility was having trouble breaking through to a concept of his contribution. We had identified his principal customers in terms of their needs for his services. Then he began to ask himself what common thread he could find that formed his contribution. Initially he said, "We provide the highest possible system availability for the keyboard users, and we provide the best possible software systems for managers who need computer support."

My response was, "It seems to me that service availability is an *attribute* of your contribution. What is the contribution itself? Software systems are means to an end. What is the end?" Finally, the figurative light bulb went off over his head. "I think," he said, "that the contribution of data processing is *empowerment*. We empower people, through information, to accomplish their missions." That immediately led him to issues like service responsiveness, customer education, cooperativeness, and ease of doing business. Because many data processing departments have acquired reputations as slow, unresponsive, and bureaucratic in their dealings with customer departments, he decided to rethink the whole concept of his organization's role.

This kind of thinking can produce some exciting results and often leads to a redirection of the focus of attention and activity. Your departmental contribution may be very clear to you, or it may require some careful thought to make it clear.

Bear in mind that you must have it clearly in *your* head before you can teach it and dramatize it to your staff. Work on it until you can express it in simple, meaningful, compelling terms. Then you can cast it in the form of a mission statement and make that mission statement the foundation of your whole operation.

DUAL MISSIONS: SERVICE AND POLICING

In thinking about your mission, bear in mind that you may have two distinct aspects of your contribution. One, of course, is your *service mission*. This is the contribution you make to helping other people and groups accomplish their missions. But you may also have a second kind of mission, a *policing mission*. You have to make the two of them compatible.

A policing mission is a role you have of advocating, preserving, or defending a certain cause in the organization at large. For example, a personnel department usually finds itself advocating such values as equal employment opportunity, observance of labor laws, elimination of sexual harassment, quality of work life, employee development by managers, and the like. These issues may affect the customer departments less in a service frame of reference and more in a policing frame of reference.

Similarly, a purchasing department has an advocacy mission of getting the highest value for the company's money. Purchasing experts can use their special methods such as quantity purchases, preferred-customer pricing, competitive procurement, and special sourcing to get the best deals. The typical customer department would not have the knowledge, expertise, or procedures to handle the acquisition of major purchases these ways.

The legal department, if the organization has one, also has a dual role of service and advocacy. In addition to rendering legal services to customer departments, it must advocate legally prudent businesses practices. It must oppose actions by managers who would commit the company to significant legal or financial exposure without the proper safeguards. Customer departments could innocently create severe problems by unilateral action; the legal department has the right, through its advocacy or policing mission, to make its voice heard.

The key point in thinking about your service mission and your policing mission in the same breath is to make them compatible and not mutually exclusive or antagonistic. This offers quite a challenge in some cases. In the example of the purchasing department, there can often be a conflict between all-out service to the purchasing customer and the purchasing department's mission of getting value for money. For example, some purchasing departments become rigid and bureaucratic in dealing with their customers, giving the impression they care only about their policing mission.

When the purchasing department insists on preparing a competitive procurement package for the smallest purchase or refuses to recognize the customer department's contention that only one supplier really has the product or expertise needed or refuses to expedite the process no matter what kind of case the customer puts up, they are not contributing; they are obstructing.

When the people in the legal department act like they are too important to talk to ordinary working people and deal only with the highest executive levels, they are obstructing, not contributing. When everything takes weeks and months, as they get around to it when they get good and ready, they don't come across as being in the service business. The advocacy mission contaminates the service mission.

In an effective internal service department, the service mission and the advocacy mission go hand in hand. The manager tries at all times to maintain a sense of balance between value and convenience for the customer and proper attention to the cause he or she must advocate.

WORK WITH YOUR KEY PEOPLE, NOT AROUND THEM

As you begin to develop or redevelop the conceptual basis for your department's role, be sure to bring your subordinate managers and other key people into your thinking. Your managerial style may not necessarily be highly democratic, and this doesn't have to be a democratic process. But bear in mind that they will eventually have to understand, believe in, and sell the mission to everyone in the organization. It stands to reason that they will feel more comfortable with the direction if they played a significant part in establishing it.

And for your own part, remember that the thinking process that gives rise to your mission is a fairly complicated and creative one. Even if you intend to reserve for yourself the final say in setting direction and expressing it in finished form, you need the benefit of their thinking. They work with the customer and the organizational processes every day, and they see where the problems are. They know what irritates the customers and what pleases. They have a good sense of the customers' problems, needs, and priorities. It only makes sense to capitalize on the brain power and experience available to you.

HOW TO BUILD A MISSION STATEMENT

Now you are ready to formulate a mission statement, which is a written expression of the contribution your department makes, in operational terms, to the success of the organization. This stage requires a bit of conceptual thinking, the ability to balance generalities and specifics, and a bit of journalistic competence.

Your objective is to come up with a clear, meaningful, nontrivial, compelling, and actionable statement of purpose. A good mission statement, in my view, tells three things:

1. Who the customer or beneficiary of the service is.
2. The value or contribution provided to that customer.
3. The special means and circumstances of providing the service.

I would prefer not to suggest specific wordings of actual mission statements because I don't want to contribute to a "formula" type approach. However, it does seem necessary to give a few hypothetical mission statements that might serve as starting points for a few selected internal departments. How about a mission statement for a computer department that says something like:

We empower executives, managers, and working people in this organization to accomplish their objectives through information, by providing highly reliable, up-to-date, responsive data processing services, equipment, and technical support.

Perhaps no data processing executive would want to take this draft mission statement verbatim, but I believe it has the basic ingredients. It has a focus: the customers, people who have their own missions to accomplish. It has an organizing principle: empowering people through information. And it has the means: highly available data processing resources and the technical expertise to help customers meet their needs.

How about a mission statement for a public relations department? It might go something like this:

We assist company leaders in all key areas of the operation to reach the appropriate publics with their messages, and by providing advice, assistance, and know-how we enable them to communicate their messages with the desired impact.

Not perfect, maybe, and maybe it wouldn't satisfy all PR managers, but it does suggest a way of expressing what the department does in terms of the benefits it offers its customers.

Let's try one more, this time a safety department. It might read something like this:

We enable people to work safely and without fear of injury everywhere in company facilities, by enhancing safety awareness, providing education, training, and equipment, and providing special expertise in safety analysis and accident prevention.

One can certainly argue for other ways of expressing these mission statements, and certainly there is no "correct" form or format. A mission statement is, after all, the product of the manager's own point of view about the contribution of the department. However, there are some features or characteristics that I feel make for an effective statement. They are:

1. It is reasonably brief.
2. It dwells on the value delivered to the customer.
3. It explains the means for its accomplishment, but does not go into detail about specific activities.
4. It does not deal in platitudes or "motherhoods."
5. It is reasonably focused in its description of the service.
6. It is actionable; i.e., it suggests broad lines of action necessary for its achievement.
7. The department to which it applies can be held accountable for its accomplishment; it explains what *that group* hopes to accomplish.

Note that in the three examples of mission statements given the *customer* is the one described as meeting the ultimate objective. In other words, the data processing department hopes to empower its customers by means of information and expertise, not solve their problems for them. The public relations department recognizes that it is the organization's leaders who must communicate their messages to the various publics; the PR people are the means for that communication; they do not originate or control it. And the safety department does not try to take on the mission of making the company a safe place to work; the people and their leaders must do that. Each of these departments, as seen through its mission statement, sees itself as *the means for the effectiveness of others*, not as the all-powerful keeper of the keys to information, public relations, or safety.

I hope these examples will help you get your mental machinery going as you draft your own mission statement. You'll probably find that it takes a bit of work and discussion to come up with one you feel is just about perfect. Just be sure to test each candidate against the criteria listed above. Does it tell the three key things it should? And does it meet the characteristics described for clarity and validity? If it does, and you and your key people agree that it gives the proper focus to your department's contribution, then you've probably got it.

Ultimately the mission statement should help you manage. At the Queen's Medical Center in Honolulu, support department managers use their mission statements on a regular basis to keep their units' activities focused on quality. The center's director of organization development, Angeline Twarynski, says, "Our service management approach is based strongly on middle management leadership. The mission statements are essential to getting the clarity of vision necessary to fulfill our business strategy." Bill Kennett, head of material services, says, "The service management model, and especially the mission-statement approach, has given us a much better focus for what we do. The managers in my department are turned on and excited in a way I've never seen before."

HOW TO BUILD A PHILOSOPHY STATEMENT

Some managers like to support the mission statement with a *philosophy statement*, which usually takes the form of a statement of values or beliefs or key points people should keep in mind. This, too, if used, should be brief—no more than one page—and reasonably articulate. It also needs a focus, or it can degenerate into a collection of "motherhoods" and platitudes. The best focus is usually the mission itself. In other words, the philosophy statement recognizes the mission statement as defining the purpose of the organization, and the philosophy statement expresses the values that will impel the organization in its achievement of the mission.

A philosophy statement usually tells the people in the department things like:

1. Your convictions about the importance of giving quality service to your customers.
2. Your beliefs about the primary needs and priorities of your customers.
3. Your beliefs about the ways people should work to meet customer needs.
4. The human values you want to see playing a primary role in day-to-day work activities.
5. What the employees can expect of you and your key leaders in terms of support and enablement to them.

Note that the philosophy statement is a statement from management, just as the mission statement is. It expresses *your* decisions about the dominant values you want to see in effect. It has the specific purpose of channeling the thinking and behavior of everyone in the department toward accomplishing the mission within the parameters you consider important.

Later we will discuss ways to publish and dramatize the philosophy statement to make sure everyone understands and can respond to it.

DEVELOPING YOUR SERVICE PLAN

Your service plan tells the people in your organization what they need to do to accomplish the service mission you have established. It need not be long-winded, detailed, or elaborate. In fact, the best plan simply spells out the broad areas of effort, in terms of results expected, and leaves the doing of it up to them.

Too many organizations have "upside-down" planning processes. That is, they place too much emphasis in detail and not
enough emphasis on concept. As a result, they may have elaborate documents called plans, which represent very little real
thinking and planning. Departmental plans, in these cases, become little more than verbose explanations of the budgets they
have adopted.

They offer little in the way of rationale about the direction
the department is taking, its contribution to the welfare of the
organization, or its key priorities for accomplishment. More human effort is probably wasted in planning and budgeting than
in any other so-called management activity involved in organizational life.

A better way of "right-side-up" planning is for the department head to spell out clearly the mission, philosophy, and *key
result areas* in a brief, concise, and meaningful few pages.

After that, all units or functions in the department should
figure out how to aim their actions at that plan. Pages and
pages of description, staffing tables, and budgetary breakdowns
do little to communicate direction and often simply waste time.
In most organizations, there is a continual day-to-day process
of discussion and interaction that results in a shared understanding of the nitty-gritty work to be done. Why document in
great detail what everyone already knows? A half-dozen pages
should be plenty of room to spell out the direction.

Be sure to develop your plan in cooperation with the few
key people who report directly to you to get the benefit of their
perspectives, their knowledge of the customer and the operation, and to enlist their early support for its implementation.
Allow plenty of time for working meetings with them, in which
you talk over in depth just how you want the operation to run.
Hear what they have to say, and incorporate their best ideas
into the approach. Only after you have carefully thought through
what you want to do with your department should you move
into the process of writing up your plan. Separate the thinking
process from the writing process. Don't try to do a lot of creative thinking during the "journalistic" process. Do one first,
then the other.

The "key result area" approach is a very useful one for setting direction concisely and communicating it concisely. Key result areas are categories for accomplishment that add up directly to the fulfillment of the mission. They may change from one planning period to the next, depending on the relative emphasis you choose to give to your department's activities. It is generally best to choose key result areas that reflect change, growth, and development in your department's capabilities and service contribution, rather than ones which merely describe routine activities that are already underway.

Keep the number of key result areas small, and choose them carefully. Three is a good number. Four or five may be manageable. But when you get beyond that number, you tend to diffuse energy and confuse people about what really counts. Seven or eight key result areas are too many for people to pay attention to. It is much better to focus very strongly on only two or three areas throughout a year's work, rather than try to get people to work on a multitude of priorities, none of which really get the attention they deserve.

For each key result area, or "KRA," if you like, decide what kinds of efforts you'd like to see going on. Think of the various tasks, developmental projects, and special systems you want to get going. What will it take for this KRA to really come alive? What are the priorities within this particular category? What really counts? How will you know how well your unit is doing in this area? Do this kind of preliminary thinking for all of the KRAs you have established.

The next step after working out the various key result areas is to set one or more *critical objectives* in each area. Again, avoid the temptation to have too many markers in your plan, or no one will pay attention to any of them. Try to focus on just one important goal for each KRA. If you find this just too narrow and confining, set other goals as necessary. But don't set up 15 or 20 goals, or you'll end up with just another bureaucratic papermill.

Make the plan simple and focused enough that you can work the plan throughout the year. Don't let it get out of hand. In setting a goal for any KRA, remember to make it simple, specific, concrete, attainable, and measurable—at least in qualitative terms. Make sure it's a "natural" goal, i.e., one that makes immediate sense to people and especially one that is sensible to the people who have to work to achieve it.

Once you feel fairly confident about the thinking process and you have your mission, philosophy, key result areas, and critical objectives well in hand, you are ready to put your ideas for the department into writing and begin orienting your people in the direction you want to go.

ALIGNMENT: MAKING SURE YOUR PLAN MATCHES THE BIG PICTURE

Before you go much further with the development and publication of your departmental direction, it's usually a good idea to confer with your boss and make sure he or she understands what you're trying to do. Your direction must fit in with the big picture of the overall organization.

Presumably you've had numerous discussions with your boss concerning the mission and priorities of the parent organization, and you have received some guidance about the direction of your unit. And, presumably, you've incorporated the boss's mission, philosophy, and priorities into the concept of your unit's direction. Now it's time to test your direction to make sure it fits in with the higher level direction and make sure your approach is valid in the overall organizational context.

Ask your boss to review your direction with you in draft form—the mission, philosophy, key result areas, and critical objectives. Make sure you have his or her undivided attention at some mutually convenient time. Explain in your own words what you're trying to do, and then ask the boss to read and react to your write-up.

During this critical process of achieving consensus with your boss, be willing to adapt to his or her input. If you walk in with your whole approach set in concrete, and you're unwilling to rethink it or listen to alternative approaches, you're programing the situation for frustration. If you have concerns about getting the boss's overall endorsement of the approach, it might make sense to include him or her more deeply in the development process. In such a case, it may help to have the boss work closely with you in working things out, so you'll be more sure of a sale when you present it in semifinal form.

If you're basically confident about getting acceptance of your approach, then just be sure you're willing to make modest changes or adjustments in order to honor the boss's inputs. He or she might not insist on any particular wording or structure for the guidance documents, but there may be certain areas that should reflect his or her views very directly.

You might also want to discuss your departmental approach with a few other key managers at your level to get the benefit of their perspectives. Don't ask them to rewrite your direction, just to react to it and suggest improvements if they have any.

This can be a very good way to presell them on the direction you'll be taking and the relationship of your department to theirs, as well to get good ideas for refining your concept of your internal business.

Don't rule out the possibility that your boss or colevel managers may suggest a revision of your thinking that may be more valid. Be open-minded and prepared to listen to other ways of going about your mission if they can point out flaws in your thinking. It could happen that, with the best of intentions, you and your key advisers have been too narrow and parochial in your thinking. Others, who are not so personally committed to the problems and issues of your department, might be able to set you onto a line of thinking that could eventually make much more sense in terms of your accomplishment. Remaining open to those possibilities can help you get a better solution, and it will probably reduce your frustration level as well.

In short: don't develop your direction in a vacuum. Seek the wise counsel of others. Listen to your customers. Listen to your boss. Listen to your key advisers. They all may have something to contribute. In the end, the direction you set is really up to you, but be sure it makes good organizational sense and that it's valid in terms of its contribution to the business.

CHAPTER 9

ORIENTING THE PEOPLE FOR INTERNAL SERVICE

Habit is habit, and not to be tossed out the window by any
man; but coaxed down the stairs one step at a time.

—*Mark Twain*

WRITING AND PUBLISHING YOUR PLAN

Make the publication of your plan an act of communication,
persuasion, and motivation, not an exercise in bureaucracy.
Decide at the very beginning, before you dot the last *i* or cross
the last *t*, that it will be a living plan and not just another
administrative document that collects cobwebs in a file cabinet
somewhere.

This means that you need to invest the proper effort in
making it journalistically effective. It must be clear, concise,
simple, informative, and compelling. It must help people understand the direction of the organization and the broad outlines
of the march you are asking them to undertake. If you are a
reasonably competent writer, it is probably best that you write
the plan personally. It needs your personal touch. Each part
needs to reflect the intensity of your personal commitment and
the special style of operating you want to embrace.

If you have trouble getting the subject matter into simple,
compelling prose, choose a skilled "wordsmith" who understands the basic ideas and have that person prepare a draft.
Don't be reluctant to revise, revise, and revise again. Keep it
focused on the key points you want to get across, but make sure
it comes out in clear, compelling language.

You may want to consider a general format roughly like this:

1. Cover page.
2. Table of contents.
3. The mission statement.
4. The philosophy statement.
5. Three to five key result areas for the planning period.
6. A general indication of actions within each key result area.

Try to keep the whole thing rather brief, perhaps a half-dozen pages total. Consider having it attractively produced, say in "desktop publishing" form, on high quality paper, and bound in some sort of special folder or booklet form. Give it the attention it deserves, because you'll be asking people to refer to it many times. A plan that is attractive to the eye conveys an extra impression of significance and importance that will help you in your efforts to dramatize the ideas it contains.

A quick reading of your plan will show whether your departmental approach is really customer focused and service oriented. Are you spending most of your resources on accomplishing the mission, rather than on serving your own department's private agenda? Are you deploying your people for maximum impact on your customer needs? Are you acquiring new equipment for direct improvements in your service capability, rather than to pursue your own private hobbies?

 ## ORIENTING YOUR KEY PEOPLE

The first step in rolling out your service plan is to share it with your key people—the ones you rely on to get things done in your organization. Depending on the size of your unit and the range of your responsibilities, you may have subordinate managers who look after various functional areas. If you don't, you probably have one or more key people in your group with whom you work most closely to get things done. In any case, work closely with your key action people to make sure they understand it and can commit their energies to it.

Of course, you should have been developing the mission concept and the plan in conjunction with them right along. They may have had more or less involvement in the process, depending on how you like to do things and the nature of your unit's structure and activities. But in any case, they should have had at least some opportunity to offer their ideas, opinions, perceptions, and suggestions for the direction and the mission. And they should have had some degree of input into the thinking process that led to the setting of the key result areas and the critical goals.

To start with, have a meeting with your key people, and give each of them a copy of the plan. Take them through it page by page, and make sure they understand every word of it. Ask them, one by one, whether they understand it. Does the mission statement make sense? Can they act on it? Does the philosophy make sense? Can they adhere to it? Ask whether they have any personal reservations about making the plan the center of attention for all that they do. Be sure to deal with all of their concerns candidly, straightforwardly, and positively. Especially, don't brush aside anyone's apprehensions or doubts. Draw out all objections and concerns and work through them constructively.

A note of caution: don't allow the meeting to degenerate into a gripe session about "the way things are around here." You probably won't hear much of this, but sometimes there can be things going on in an organization that cause frustration, apprehension, or cynicism on the part of managers or key working people. Acknowledge and respect their concerns, but make sure the meeting stays on the track of implementing the service plan.

In the same vein, avoid the management gaming that can sometimes go on when people come back with, "Well, it takes money to give good service. If you'll give us more resources, we can give better service to our customers." This is often a cop-out that has nothing to do with a commitment to service. You need to remind anyone who may say such a thing that everything has to take place within an atmosphere of trade-offs and careful thinking about priorities. Don't allow side issues to contaminate the discussion of the service commitment and plan.

(1)   Next, ask each of them to explain to you how he or she sees the plan affecting his or her individual area of responsibility. Help them think through what it will mean to actually live, work, and function this way. Discuss its implications for each of the functional areas of your organization. Get into some of the details involved in the implementation. Help them identify any obstacles or issues that may need attention to pave the way for a successful mission.

(2)   Finally, ask each of your key people, "What do you need from me to help you make this plan succeed?" Listen carefully as each one answers the question in his or her own way. Make careful notes. You may not want to make unlimited promises at this point, but do be sure you understand their views about how you should be supporting them.

(3)   Use this meeting as a formal "ratification" of the plan by you and your key leaders. Decide with them on the exact steps to take as you present the plan to everyone else in the organization. Figure out a reasonable timetable and write it down. Make sure each of them gets a copy of the timetable, and make especially sure each one understands his or her involvement in the process.

(4)   You may choose to have each of your subordinate managers, if you have them, personally carry the plan to their people; or you may choose to take the lead yourself and communicate the plan to everyone. Whichever avenue you choose, don't go around your key people or leave them out of the process. Make up your mind to work with and through them, not around them. For that reason, it is important that they know exactly what they have to do, when, and how.

DRAMATIZING THE SERVICE MISSION

Communicating your departmental direction effectively calls for a bit of flair, possibly even a bit of drama. If you don't put some energy into it and if you don't make it something special in people's minds, it will come across as just another piece of paper to be filed away. The surest way to consign your mission statement to oblivion is to hand out copies of it to everyone and do nothing else. As important as it may be to you, it will only be as important to them as you make it.

How you dramatize the mission depends mostly on the number of people you have to reach with it. If you have a small band of a half-dozen people or so, or even if your group numbers as many as 15 or 20, it's a fairly easy matter to get them all together for a meeting. If you head a department of dozens of people or a division with hundreds or even thousands of staff, it's a somewhat different matter.

However, you can approach the job of reaching a large number of people as just a repeat version of reaching a small number if you work through your subordinate managers to get the message out. In other words, you can orient your managers thoroughly and then give them the task of carrying out the orientation through their respective departmental units. That's a natural way to keep them in their proper role as leaders. It's your message, but they teach and preach it.

Let's spell out a general approach to a mission-orientation session for a natural-sized work group, with the group leader as the person handling the session. Then we can see how to extend that process to a large organization by having individual group meetings for the various areas. Assume for a moment that one of your subordinate managers is working with his or her group. If you're the head of a small group, the process is pretty much the same, except that you're presenting your own message.

The manager in charge of the group calls a meeting of all staff for a convenient time and at a convenient place. The "scuttlebutt" preceding the meeting lets people know that it's to be an unusual occurrence at which new plans are to be shared.

Make sure the grapevine doesn't start sending messages about layoffs, the company being bought out, or a reorganization. The anticipation should be that the meeting will present something important and positive.

The manager should be thoroughly prepared for the presentation. This includes plenty of copies of the employee booklet or pamphlet, i.e., whatever form you've chosen to present the new mission, philosophy, and general direction. If the group is larger than about 10 people, the manager should probably have a few overhead transparencies and a projector to help present the information. If the manager is somewhat uncomfortable with group presentations, he or she should probably have a well-structured agenda to follow.

The meeting should be relatively brief, it should move along snappily, and it should stick to the subject. But at the same time, it needs a sense of occasion—a few touches that make it special. One way to do this is to serve refreshments of some kind, especially something rather unusual. Having a senior executive present also helps to lend significance to the occasion.

If you are a divisional executive and your subordinate manager is presenting your mission and direction, you may want to offer some comments at the start of the meeting to reinforce the importance of the message.

Some organizations like to add a touch of imagination or humor to such an event. The president of Santa Monica Hospital Medical Center, Len LaBella, took this approach when he introduced his service philosophy several years ago. He had evolved the idea of using a cartoon-style hippopotamus as a metaphor for the abbreviation "HiPO," which stood for "high performance organization." He had established the order of the HiPO, with T-shirts, sweatshirts, and watches all bearing the cartoon of a cuddly hippo.

Since it was a medical organization, he established the "HiPO-cratic oath" with an appropriate award certificate. As a consultant to the organization, I was properly inducted into the order. Over the years, my office has become a repository for some of the most outrageous gadgets, prizes, and memorabilia of organizational programs. I wouldn't part with any of them.

There are many ways you can find to make a mission meeting a memorable event, once you decide to use your imagination. The Australian Gas Light company hired the Darling Harbour Convention Center in Sydney for an all-employees evening program. Chief Executive Len Bleasel said, "We decided to make this the most important event in this decade of the company's history. We wanted people to remember this and feel good about it for years to come."

The AGL program started with refreshments and drinks and included brief talks by the chairman of the board, the chief executive, and myself as a consultant and "friend of the company." Each employee received a small booklet explaining the new mission and direction of the company. Then followed a roll-out of a new advertising campaign, which the employees got to see before it ever hit public television screens. There was also a professionally prepared video message, dramatizing the company mission from the customer's point of view. Then there was a program of music and dancing. Over 2,000 employees and their partners attended the event. It was memorable, indeed.

Returning to the small-scale introduction, which is the more typical type of event, we can still find ways to liven up the proceedings. How about a cake specially decorated for the occasion? How about cookies with a special logo or symbol of the service concept you want to portray? How about a prize drawing, open only to those who can write the mission statement from memory at the close of the meeting? How about a hired entertainer or small group who do a skit that dramatizes the mission? How about inviting a few key internal customers to share the event and encourage your employees to take up the service mission?

In presenting the mission and direction, the manager must very carefully focus on the future opportunity and not give the impression of criticizing or diminishing the group's contributions in the past. The message should be, "We've had our ways of working in the past, and we've done a pretty good job. And now we need to increase our focus on service quality and become even more aware of and responsive to the customer's needs. We want to deliver a high-quality service we can all be proud of."

It's also important, after presenting the direction to your staff, that you give them some idea of what's going to happen next. They will be asking, either aloud or in their minds, "How, if at all, will life be different from now on?" You need some good answers to give them. This ties into the approaches suggested in following chapters, in which you begin to align or realign the customer-impact systems in your organization.

Give them a general description of the process you plan to follow over the next some months and years, in which you will support the process of their managers working with them to improve the service systems.

And finally, allow for questions, comments, and feedback. Make the occasion primarily ceremonial in nature, with the emphasis on the presentation. Don't encourage people to nit-pick the wording of the mission statement or the philosophy or to bring up side-issues or special-interest problems; stick to the gist of the matter. But do listen openly to their questions and concerns. This isn't a griping session, but you mustn't make it just a one-way push. They should leave feeling they understand the direction and that you understand them.

Back to the matter of large-scale rollout in a sizable department or division, the simplest and most controllable method is to have all of the individual department or unit heads conduct orientation sessions with their respective staff members. As mentioned above, you might want to attend each of these sessions, although it's probably best to leave that to the discretion of the individual managers.

If you choose the method of the unit-by-unit rollout, make sure every one of the managers can handle the job of presenting the mission and direction. If you suspect that any of your managers is not fully on board with you, psychologically as well as circumstantially, consider having a private discussion with that person to clear away any concerns or problems. If you really feel the manager can't or won't support the direction, then you have a responsibility to consider carefully that person's role in the organization.

Have a kit of materials prepared for your managers to use in their sessions. Make enough copies so each of them can have one.

For those who may have difficulty making presentations, work with them ahead of time, or make someone from the training department available to help them dry-run the session. Don't skimp on this kind of preparation; it can be the difference between a ho-hum implementation of your concept and a really high-impact implementation.

ORIENTING NEWCOMERS TO YOUR ORGANIZATION

If you really believe in the direction you've set for the organiza-tion, then you'll have to be prepared to sell it and resell it at every opportunity. This includes especially selling it to new people who come to work with your group. Orienting the new person properly on Day One is critical to giving continuity to your concept and making sure it has staying power.

Make it a requirement that every single person who comes to work in your organization will get an explanation of the mission and direction within, say, five days after coming on board. The first day is probably too soon because the newcomer typ-ically won't even know the basics. But don't let it go more than a few days. If you do, you lose the element of newness that can have a big impact on the person's thinking. Also, you run the risk of having his or her attitudes contaminated by coworkers who may not fully share the vision. They need to hear it fresh, new, and unadulterated from the horse's mouth.

If you have a small organization, you should do the indi-vidual orientation personally, of course. If it's a large group, have your subordinate managers do it; you may want to have a meeting or your own with the newcomer just to reinforce the message in your own way. If you have a large organization, resist the temptation to wait until you have enough new hires and orient them in "batches." It's fine to have an employee ori-entation for newcomers; every company of any size needs to do this. But make sure your new employees understand the direc-tion of *your* department the very first week they come to work.

So far as the orientation method goes, it can be fairly sim-ple, but it should be relatively formal and impactful. It should take place in the form of a special meeting with the newcomer's manager, and this should be the only subject of the discussion. Again, you might want to provide the manager with a kit of materials for convenience. The employee should receive a per-sonal copy of your mission booklet or pamphlet with the expec-tation that he or she will keep it and be able to produce it when asked.

And don't assume that the orientation will stick just because you do it early. Ideas like this require repetition and reinforcement. For example, it might make sense for the newcomer's boss to conduct an initial first-week orientation and for you to have a meeting with that person during the second week of employment. Thereafter, the manager can orient the new person to his or her job responsibilities by using the mission and direction as a way to explain priorities.

And even after that, you'll still need ways to remind people of the direction and to reinforce it in various concrete ways, as explained in a later chapter.

CHAPTER 10

ALIGNING THE SYSTEMS FOR INTERNAL SERVICE

Great ideas need landing gear as well as wings.
—*C. D. Jackson*

Once you have your mission clearly defined and you have begun to make it real and tangible for the people in your organization, you can begin aligning or realigning the systems you and your people use to deliver your service product. As I have pointed out several times in the early part of this book, and indeed in the books *Service America!* and *At America's Service*, systems are often the enemies of service.

Almost everything said in this chapter applies in the context of working with your staff to find better ways of operating, rather than in the context of your making unilateral analyses and determinations about how to improve things. Make a special effort to engage as many of your staff as possible in the process of searching for service quality problems and solving them.

PINPOINTING YOUR CUSTOMER-IMPACT SYSTEMS

Start by identifying your *customer-impact systems*. A customer-impact system is any process or apparatus that affects your customer more or less directly in the form of some kind of moment of truth. Remembering that a moment of truth is any episode in which your (internal) customer comes into contact with any aspect of your operation and gets an impression of your service, you can easily identify these systems.

A system, in this context, is not only a physical arrangement of resources, such as a reception or waiting area, a computer system, or a physical materials handling system. It can also mean a set of information-handling procedures, a sequence of employee actions that involve the customer, or indeed any rule-based flow of events.

The easiest way to identify your customer-impact systems is simply to go back to the list of moments of truth you compiled in your original analysis of your customer interface, as described in a previous chapter. Each of those moments of truth will point you to some process that goes on in your organization that deserves careful study.

A very simple example: a manager or staff member from a customer department places a telephone call to your department, perhaps asking to talk to you. You are not in at the time of the call, so someone—presumably—takes a message for you and gives it to you when you return. You return the call. The means for carrying out that simple little sequence of events is a customer-impact system.

This example may sound moronically simple until you consider how many possibilities it offers to create or destroy an impression of quality service. Suppose, for instance, that the employee fails to get the caller's full name and writes you a note to call Mary in Engineering. You may not know a Mary in Engineering, even though the staff member assumed you do. Now you have to call the number and hope there is only one Mary there.

Suppose the staff member made a mistake on the telephone extension: for example, by transposing digits or getting one digit wrong. In a large organization with a huge number of phone lines, you might not be able to track down the caller. After about a week, Mary assumes you don't care about her problem.

Suppose the person taking the message forgets to give it to you or place it in your message slot immediately, then goes out to lunch, gets an upset stomach from some diabolical chili, and has to go home early. Suppose it's a Friday. The person recovers by Monday and about midmorning discovers the message on his or her desk. It was relatively urgent on Friday morning, but the caller has the impression it wasn't urgent to you.

At the risk of belaboring a very simple example, I submit that there are no trivial customer-impact systems in an organization. Virtually all of them can cause problems for you or your customer if they don't operate effectively.

Let's look at another very simple customer-impact system. Let's say one of your customer managers wanders into your departmental offices, hoping to talk to someone who can give some advice or assistance on a matter relating to your group's responsibility. He really should have telephoned, but he was in your neighborhood and decided to drop in. When he walks in, all three of your staff members whose desks are in sight are occupied with telephone calls. He stands there for quite a while, hoping somebody will notice him and react, but nobody does.

Maybe you're really not set up for "walk-in" business. You don't have an actual reception area, and you haven't appointed anybody in particular to meet and greet people who wander in. Nevertheless your customer feels uncomfortable, unwelcome, and unserved. None of the people on the telephones see it as their responsiblity to interrupt what they're doing or even to acknowledge his presence.

In a similar fashion, he might happen to wander in when no one is occupying any of the desks he can see. He doesn't know what to do, so he wanders around until he spots somebody he can talk to. He makes his needs known, but that person is unaccustomed to such an event and doesn't know what to do. Does the staff person say, "You'll have to come back later, when so-and-so is here"?

Or does he or she say, "I'm sorry; I don't know how to help you, and so-and-so isn't here right now. May I take your name and telephone number and have him give you a call as soon as possible? Would you like me to write down a few words about the problem you need help with? Can you tell me a good time to call when you'll be in your office?"

There is a big difference, isn't there? Often the only reason why customers—especially internal customers—get poor treatment is that the staff person simply doesn't know what to do.

This is where a positive attitude comes in, supported by a clear understanding of the organization's service mission and philosophy. In the one case, the employee is tempted to brush off the customer and try to get rid of him because he or she is caught off guard, embarrassed at not knowing what to say or do and sees the customer as an interruption to the work at hand. In the other case, knowing your philosophy and the mission for service, the employee makes the best of the situation by using common sense on behalf of the customer. Such a person is trained to view the customer not as a nuisance or an intrusion but as a person who has a right to receive cordial treatment and the benefit of the employee's undivided attention for a few minutes.

This, again, is one of your customer-impact systems, however simple. What are the parts of the system? The office space, the people who work closest to the entrance, and the rules—conscious or unconscious—that govern their behavior toward outsiders.

From these simple examples, you can progress to more and more complex customer-impact systems, but they all tend to have certain things in common. These common factors include:

1. They are systems you and your staff have set up, either knowingly or unknowingly.
2. They are not necessarily familiar, logical, or comprehensible to your customers who don't work with them every day.
3. They probably support the convenience of your department's activities first and the convenience of your customers second.

What you must do is examine every one of these customer-impact systems from the customer's point of view. What does it look like to the customer? What are its apparent priorities, as seen through the customer's eyes? How does the customer access the system, and how does it affect his or her activities?

It helps to "be" a customer, at least mentally, for some period of time and try to exercise your systems with hypothetical needs or problems. By mentally walking through these processes, you can discover a great deal about the underlying rationales for their design and about their influence on your customers' perceptions.

IDENTIFYING HIGH-PAYOFF SYSTEM IMPROVEMENTS

If you have a relatively large or complex departmental operation, you may be surprised to see how many different processes you need to look at on behalf of your customer. In such a case it helps to prioritize the agenda of improvements by selecting certain systems for initial attention. The best candidates for early evaluation are those that seem to offer the best payoff in terms of improved service quality, cost reduction, and—preferably—both.

In looking for your high-payoff system improvements, again in close consultation with the people of your organization, go back to your customer research. Look at the processes your customers seem unhappy about. Which area causes the most complaints?

For example, a medical records department in a hospital used this approach to pinpoint the systems it used to get patient data to the physician in preparation for surgery. They had some really hostile "docs" whenever a patient's file did not arrive at the surgery suite by 7 A.M. along with the patient and the surgeon who had scheduled it for an operation.

In analyzing the processes, we discovered that the records were frequently held up as they circulated from one department to another in conjunction with the various preoperative tests and procedures. If the patient underwent a test the afternoon before surgery, the records might not get back to the medical records department that day.

We isolated this communication system as a primary area of high payoff in terms of the physician's perceptions of service.

It also directly affected the perceptions of the ultimate customer. Imagine how you'd feel if they wheeled you down to the surgery department, had you lie there on a gurney for an hour, and then told you the surgery had been postponed because they couldn't find your records.

In the same hospital we found a number of physician complaints about the department that had responsibility for delivering surgical instruments and supplies to the operating room. They used a "case-cart" system, which meant that they prepared a roll-away cart, complete with all of the items typically needed for a particular type of surgery, which they knew were needed because they had the surgery schedule for that day.

Problems sometimes occurred when they sent the wrong kind of cart for a particular surgery or when they accidentally left out one or more of the needed items. Additionally, if a doctor encountered an unexpected problem during surgery and suddenly called for a special item of equipment, it could take as long as five minutes or more—an eternity during a surgical procedure—for the supply people to get the item up to the operating room.

Given the fact that a normal surgical procedure is a fairly serious and stressful matter, it was not surprising that the doctors were disturbed.

Clearly, this was a customer-impact system of major significance. An associated problem with this system was the occasional error in which a cutting instrument scheduled for sharpening was misrouted, and found its way into a new case-cart.

A surgeon who discovers, during a procedure, that a pair of surgical scissors won't cut tissue properly is not a happy camper.

Sometimes the high-payoff system improvements involve interdepartmental cooperation. You may find it necessary to team up with another department in order to get the bigger system to make sense before you can improve your own. For example, in a large aerospace firm, there is typically a complex process by which the company puts together a proposal for submission to a government agency to win a hardware development contract for, say, an airplane or a computer system. In one company, which is very typical of the industry, there was always a jam-up during the final days of the 30-day response period.

In this firm, the engineers would go to work on the design, the manufacturing people would go to work on the construction aspects of the plan, the program-management people would work out the project work plan and timetable, and the finance department would be working on the cost estimate. All of these items had to come together in a final document, usually 200 to 300 pages long, in time for delivery to the client agency. One day past the deadline and the agency would reject the proposal, which had cost the company many thousands of dollars to prepare.

The problem, typically, would arise when a project manager for a proposal would start thinking, about a week before the due date, that he should get started on the typing and production work for the document. He would stroll into the graphic arts department and say, "I've got a proposal in progress, and I'm going to need some typing and some illustration." The head of graphics would ask, "When's your due date?" and would just about faint when he discovered he had all of a week to produce a 300-page document, which the project workers had not yet finished writing. The only reason he didn't faint was that he'd had it done to him so many times he could usually see it coming.

In such a situation, the project manager is the customer of the graphics department, but graphics should also be entitled to feel like a customer as well. They can't do their job effectively if other departments don't include them in the planning and don't allow reasonable lead times for a sane production schedule.

These are, of course, just some typical examples. If you work in an organization of any size, you've surely seen cases like these and many worse ones. These are the areas of opportunity.

Look and listen to find out what bugs your department's customers, and you'll know where to start in analyzing internal service quality and looking for ways to improve it.

SERVICE BLUEPRINTING: A QUALITY ANALYSIS TOOL

One of the simplest and most powerful tools for analyzing and improving service quality is the *service blueprint*, which is a pencil-and-paper tool that helps you quickly describe what's going on in a particular operation. In this chapter, I'd like to introduce a method of service blueprinting that I have found extremely useful and one in particular that frontline working people find easy to use.

Before proceeding with this discussion, I need to make a slight historical adjustment to prevent any confusion about terminology and methods. In *Service America!*, Ron Zemke and I presented a technique called *service blueprinting* on pages 86 to 94.[1]

The particular approach we discussed arose from the work of several people, notably Ernest J. McCormick and Lynn Shostack. McCormick's book *Job Analysis: Methods and Applications* presents a step-logic diagraming method that deals with the actions the employee is supposed to take. Shostack's model, first presented in the *Harvard Business Review* as a profitability analysis, deals with time-and-motion studies and costing of service processes.

In the five years since the creation of *Service America!*, I have come to see the analysis of service systems in a very different perspective than that presented in that book. With all due respect to my first coauthor, Ron Zemke, and with respect for the work of McCormick and Shostack, I disagree with some of the underlying philosophy of the old approach to service blueprinting.

I also believe a different emphasis is appropriate if this kind of model is to be useful to frontline people rather than systems analysis experts who usually do this kind of work. I now believe that time-and-motion study approaches to service are limited in their applicability because they start with a manufacturing precept, i.e., that we can and should spell out the individual job tasks and actions in great detail. The bank teller's chart on page 90 is indicative, in my opinion, of the kind of thinking that has held back the development of service quality in banking for many years.

The chart spells out in excruciating detail every possible action the teller can and cannot take for the simple service of cashing a check. In my view, if we don't trust the teller to learn a simple thinking strategy about cashing checks and let him or her apply it with a few basic common-sense policies, then we are the ones creating the service problems. This kind of over-definition and overcontrol is the hallmark of what I called the "Harvard/General Motors" manufacturing approach in *At America's Service.*

I think we need a new and refreshingly simple approach to service blueprinting, which enables frontline people to understand what's important about the various things they do with and for the customer and which enables them to analyze those processes on their own and look for better ways to do them. The model presented here, I believe, does that.

A service blueprint includes the customer, the person or department in contact with the customer, and all the other "hand-off" departments as well. It gives you much more meaningful information than a simple employee job analysis chart. It shows the time line of moments of truth and organizational processes that have to transpire successfully for the customer to get his or her need taken care of.

An example is probably the most efficient way to explain how to draw a service blueprint. Figure 10–1 shows a blueprint for a typical internal service process inside a travel agency. It shows the key events in selling a ticket. Although this example portrays an external-customer service cycle, the blueprinting method applies just as well to internal-customer processes.

Note that the "banner," or headline part of the diagram across the top, identifies each of the "actors" in the process in question. The customer, in this particular case, is the buyer of the ticket; however, one could just as well choose to consider an internal manager as the customer, which would change the character of the diagram.

Note also that the vertical time line enables you to show various processes that may go on simultaneously as well as those that happen sequentially. As you follow the flow of events from top to bottom, you can get a good overview of everything that happens to and on behalf of the customer. You can also begin to spot parts of the process that deserve special attention in terms of improving service quality.

Now take a closer look at the column titled "Customer." What do you see there? Note that each of the events shown

FIGURE 10–1
The Service Blueprint

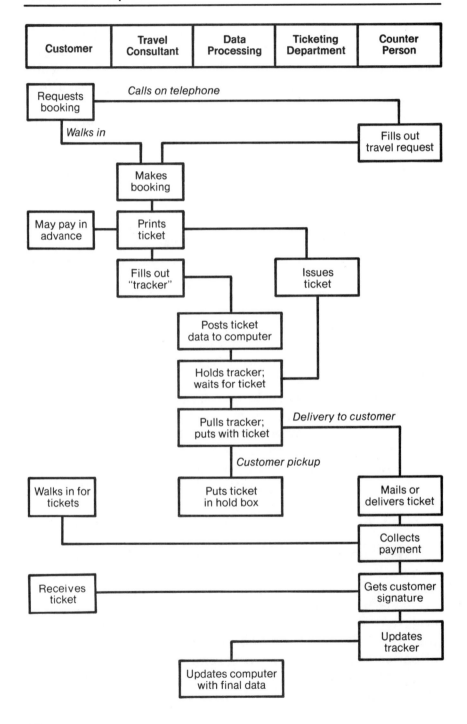

under the customer column is a *moment of truth*. In other words, it is a point at which the whole process becomes visible and tangible to the customer. Furthermore, the whole column consists of a sequence of moments of truth, which we now recognize as the *cycle of service*.

What we have in the service blueprint is a way of portraying the moments of truth and the cycle of service as the customer experiences them and at the same time a way of portraying the interplay of organizational units and functions that make up the teamwork needed to deliver a quality service experience.

It also opens the way for Service Cost Analysis, a technique that enables us to figure out how much we're actually spending on various elements of the service process.

The great value of the service blueprint, drawn in this particular format, is its role in analyzing service quality at the organizational level. By helping the various unit leaders and key service people draw up a blueprint for a certain process, you can get everybody looking at and reacting to the same picture. It immediately triggers comments and discussion about the quality of the process. People begin to see right away how complex the process is, and how, in many cases, it leaves the final responsibility for customer satisfaction up in the air.

Here are some of the most obvious questions to ask in reviewing a service blueprint:

1. How long does the entire process take?
2. How many steps are involved?
3. How many units or functions get involved?
4. Who looks after the moments of truth?
5. Who sets up the customer's expectations and how?
6. Can we speed up the process somehow?
7. Can we eliminate some of the steps?
8. How do we make sure the hand-offs work properly?
9. Can we reduce the number of players in the act?
10. Who manages the final moment of truth?
11. How can we reduce the cost of the service?

Once you have everyone agreeing on what is actually happening in a particular service process—which may be a problem in itself—you can proceed to look for ways to improve it.

HOW TO GET GREAT IMPROVEMENT IDEAS
FROM YOUR STAFF

It's customary to say that the frontline people, who live with the day-to-day service processes, are the best ones to find ways to improve those processes. That is true in some ways and not true in others. Frontline people typically *don't* come up with suggestions for improvement on their own, for several reasons.

First, it is likely that nobody has asked them to, and they don't think it is their place to question what their supervisors have told them to do. A working person typically comes into the job, gets oriented to the place, gets handed a job description or an explanation of the work he or she must do, and that's that.

There is very seldom any suggestion that the newcomer should actively look for better ways to do the job. The implication is that the managers are smart enough to know the best way of doing things, and if they designed the job this way, this must be the best way.

Second, staff people often don't have a good grasp of the big picture of the operation, again because nobody has explained to them what goes on beyond the confines of their individual jobs. It's difficult for a person to suggest improvement in a process when they only know their own little part in it. They don't know who handles a matter before they get it, and they don't know who reacts to it after they pass it along. The "manufacturing" management philosophy doesn't consider it important for the worker to know such things.

And third, staff people seldom suggest improvements because they typically haven't had much experience with problem-solving and creative-thinking methods. They've been following their job descriptions for so long that they simply aren't in the habit of looking for better ways of doing things. Without some skills and practice in looking at processes in fresh ways, it's no wonder most of them have trouble visualizing anything but the status quo.

So how do you get great ideas from your staff? Simply by making them the ones who do the analysis and asking them to be the ones to suggest better ways of delivering the service.

Rather than have a bunch of methods experts go in and analyze the operation, the trick is to teach the employees to use simple pencil-and-paper techniques like the service blueprint just described and support them in the process of applying those tools.

Depending on the size of your organization, you can have a few people involved in process improvement, or you can have many. It makes sense to start out with an educational process that includes everybody, in which they can learn about the service mission and philosophy, and they can learn how to pinpoint service processes and blueprint them as outlined above.

There are various ways you can organize this type of effort, but don't try to overorganize it. Allow it to have a kind of "one-off" ad hoc type of character. You might have one small group do a brainstorming process to identify as many service systems and processes as possible that need attention. Then allow people to form working groups or task forces and assign them various systems to work on. Just make sure they have enough training and organizational familiarity to use the service blueprinting method and that the working group has the proper representation from various functional groups.

If you have a number of these task forces, consider appointing one person to support them in their activities. This person should stay in regular touch with them, sit in on some of their analysis and problem-solving meetings, and go to work to get special assistance or technical expertise to them if they need it.

If you manage a small group, you can function as the de facto task force leader yourself. Get the whole group together on a regular basis to work on service quality issues. Identify and prioritize the systems you want to improve, and then go to work on them one at a time. Blueprint each one, or have one or two people work out a blueprint and bring it to the meeting and go from there. Put the blueprint up on the wall, and use it as a guide as you work with your people to identify ways to improve the quality of the service process and also reduce the cost.

Don't make all of this a formal, ceremonial process. Approach it informally, openly, candidly, and in the spirit of constructive change. Make sure everyone has a chance to share his or her views and ideas. Make sure you don't dominate the thinking process, even if you feel you have more knowledge or expertise than the others. Mobilize their best ideas and capitalize on their creativity. You'll find there is a double payoff in that you'll get better solutions, and they'll be more committed to the solutions they've helped to invent.

HOW TO IMPLEMENT IMPROVEMENTS SMOOTHLY

Once you have identified the kind of service system focus you want for your organization and you have pinpointed and analyzed your key customer-impact systems, you can begin making the necessary changes to realign them with your mission and direction. Bear in mind, however, that changing systems can often cause your service quality to *decline* initially instead of increase.

Don't expect to make system changes, other than minor ones, without mishaps. Keep in mind that your people have probably been working with the present systems and mechanisms for a long time, and they have grown accustomed to them. People sometimes tend to cherish even the most insanely illogical systems once they've become thoroughly conditioned to them. The most obviously superior changes can sometimes meet with surprising resistance at first.

Remember, too, that your customers may have become accustomed to the old way of doing things. They might not always like the systems, but at least they've learned to deal with them. They know how to manipulate, jockey, and generally outwit your bureaucracy, and they might not necessarily like the idea of having to figure out how to do it in a totally new way.

Nor can you be sure your customers will see changes in your way of operating as intended for their benefit. They may be skeptical at first, and they may become confused by your attempts to make things better. Not having had the benefit of your thinking process, they may view the confusion induced by system changes as merely a symptom of disorganization and lack of direction.

And, finally, expect that your staff members will experience at least some initial discomfort and confusion with any new way of doing things. They have to learn new habits, unlearn old ones, establish new hand-off mechanisms, handle information in different ways, set up new checks and balances to prevent errors, and still get the day's work done while they're changing to the new procedures. This takes time and a bit of patience.

Here are some pointers for making system changes go somewhat more smoothly:

1. Prepare your staff well in advance for the changes; help them get set up for the new way of operating.
2. Have meetings to figure out how to prevent problems during the changeover. Brainstorm for unforeseen problems or customer issues that nobody has yet considered.
3. Try to let your customers know in advance what will be happening.
4. If it's a large-scale system change, consider starting it on a pilot basis to make sure you have most of the kinks worked out of it. Then carefully advance it to the next stages.
5. Appoint a few people who will help facilitate the change by explaining, encouraging, helping, and problem-solving.
6. Be personally involved for the first week or two to observe the effects of the changes and to pitch in and help if necessary.
7. Have early and frequent progress reviews with your key people to spot any major problems before they develop too far.
8. Stay in close contact with your key customers during this stage, so you can solve any unexpected problems and let them know you're tuned in to their needs.

USING QUALITY SERVICE TEAMS

Quality teams, quality circles, service circles—call them what you like, but more and more companies are using employee-led problem-solving task groups as a way of finding better ways to deliver the service product. British Airways calls them Customer-First Teams. National Westminster Bank in England calls them QSATs, or Quality Service Action Teams. Whatever you call them, they have enormous potential for service improvement and morale building if you set them up properly.

For this discussion, I'll just call them Quality Service Teams, or QSTs. A QST is a small group of employees, usually from three to five, or at most about seven, who get together to identify opportunities for improving specific aspects of the service interface and who work through various analysis processes to come up with recommended improvements to the operation.

The QST approach is usually simpler and easier to implement than the manufacturing-type quality circle, which generally involves extensive employee training in statistical methods and ongoing support by highly trained facilitators. QST members usually need only a basic introduction to a few pencil-and-paper tools to get them started. It does help, of course, if they have access to someone skilled in group problem-solving processes. But basically, it's a do-it-yourself process.

Typically, a group may form as a result of several people having a discussion about a certain kind of service problem. If they've all received training in the QST techniques, they can get to work on the issue they've selected. Alternatively, a manager may ask several staff members from a group to attack a particular problem.

Finding problems to work on is usually fairly easy. All they have to do is look at the customer research and identify the moments of truth and cycles of service that seem to be associated with dissatisfaction for the customers. Then they can zero in on specific problems, issues, or systems for review.

The general stages of the QST process are:

1. Select a service-quality problem to attack.
2. Gather information and analyze the problem.
3. Brainstorm options.
4. Choose a solution from the best options.
5. Prepare a presentation to management for the solution.

During the problem analysis stage, the team might develop a service blueprint diagram of the process they're studying in order to pinpoint problem areas and develop alternative processes.

As mentioned, both British Airways and National Westminster Bank have made extensive use of QST methods. In 1983 and 1985, British Air launched their Customer First Teams on a worldwide basis. Most of them were focused on the external paying customer, but many solutions centered on internal service as well. They had hundreds of teams around the world developing some very innovative approaches. The company began publishing a special newsletter to help the various teams around the system keep one another up to date on their accomplishments.

National Westminster Bank, or NatWest as the Brits affectionately call it, has recently made a huge commitment to their QSATs, or Quality Service Action Teams. According to Paul Goodstadt, head of service quality programs,

> We wanted to have a very definite carry-through for people when they came out of the basic service quality training programs. We didn't want the whole thing to fade for lack of immediate action.
>
> We launched them straightaway into the QSAT activities, virtually days after they came out of the basic one-day educational event. Participation was voluntary, but we've now had over 5,000 individual QSAT projects across all 3,000 of our branches.

I was personally impressed with the enthusiasm some NatWest employees had for the process. While I was traveling with a group of Australian executives as part of a Management Frontiers service study tour to visit various European companies, we visited NatWest for a review of their approach. Goodstadt had invited two young employees from one of the local branches to brief the group on a QSAT project they had recently completed.

We were all impressed with the enthusiasm and professionalism they displayed as they described the problem their group had selected, the methods they had applied to it, the options they had considered, and the solution they had developed. It was clear that a valuable side benefit of this kind of effort is increased employee involvement, commitment, pride, and opportunities to develop career skills like creative problem solving, systems analysis, and even presentation skills.

Your organization doesn't have to be a huge one for the QST approach to offer value. A QST can have as few as three people. It can work on one issue at a time and report to you on recommendations as they come up. If you're large enough to need several or many QST groups, you probably need to appoint someone to serve as a supporter, guide, and possibly a circuit-riding process facilitator to keep them sharpened up on analysis skills and tools.

The ultimate objective of all of the approaches described in this chapter is, of course, to make sure the organizational systems work for service quality rather than against it. The basic concepts that underlie the very design of your service systems must reflect the mission, direction, and philosophy you've set for your group. If you know clearly who your customers are and what contribution you must make to help them accomplish their missions, then you can generally tell when your systems are lined up properly to support your purposes.

CHAPTER 11

CLOSING THE LOOP WITH REINFORCERS

O wad some power the giftie gie us,
to see oursels as ithers see us:
It would fra monie a blunder free us,
and foolish notion.

—Robert Burns

You haven't finished the job of orienting your organization to a service quality way of life until you've closed the loop around excellent performance. You must make *service quality measurement and feedback* a basic part of life and make sure the information it produces is available to and understood by everybody working there.

Measuring service quality has two very important benefits. First, it enables you as a manager to know how well your department is performing its mission. In that sense, it tells you to some extent how well you are managing.

Second, it gives the people in your organization critically needed feedback. They need to know how well they're doing in the eyes of the customer. You need to help them understand how their individual jobs contribute to the overall picture of outstanding service.

And, most importantly, you need to make sure the reward and reinforcement systems in your organization are operating to create the proper incentives that make people want to commit their energies to the cause. Closing the loop around service excellence means measurement, feedback, and reward and reinforcement of outstanding service work.

Let's approach the subject of service quality assessment and feedback from the philosophical point of view first. Service quality is an outcome—a state of affairs you want to achieve and maintain. Therefore, your measures should tell you when you're doing the right things to get there. Indeed, you need two kinds of measures, "means" factors and "ends" factors. More specifically, they are:

1. Customer perception measures.
2. Functional performance measures.

Customer perception measures are the "ends" factors, or *service quality measures*. These are the "report card" elements, i.e., the perceptible attributes of your service package that create the customer's opinion of your service quality.

Functional performance measures are the means factors, or *enabling measures*, which tell you how well you and your people are doing the necessary things to make quality service happen.

These two types of measures, ideally, should relate in something like the following way. Your customer research should be telling you what the critical service quality attributes are. These should go into your customer report card. Your customer report card, then, tells you what your service quality standards and your functional performance standards should be in order to have outstanding quality.

And, at the end of the chain of information, your service quality measurement system, or SQMS, should give you information on how well you and your people are meeting both sets of standards. You then know how your customers feel about your service and what's happening at the working level to create the service they are experiencing.

DEVELOPING APPROPRIATE SERVICE QUALITY STANDARDS

Just a few more thoughts about the overall approach to assessment and feedback, and then we'll proceed to explore methods and systems for doing it. First, here is probably the most useful piece of advice on the subject of service management: *don't go overboard on it.* You need to have discipline, efficiency, and productivity, but you don't need a bureaucracy in which people are drowning in measurements, rules, and regulations they don't pay attention to anyway.

Think in terms of "natural" measures of performance and natural standards of achievement for that performance. By natural measures, I mean criteria that people can easily understand, react to, work with, and consider appropriate to their circumstances.

Here are some features of a natural approach to quality or performance measurement:

1. It measures a process at an appropriate level of detail, i.e., not at the "micro" level of task activity and not at so broad a level that you can't make direct use of the measurement information.

2. It measures a process at a carefully chosen point that gives you "action leverage"; i.e., it enables you to have a big impact on the quality of the outcome by assuring compliance with criteria you can establish at that level.

3. It is part of a parsimonious measurement concept; i.e., you measure the very minimum number of variables required to give you a picture of the situation you can act upon. Instead of trying to measure everything in sight, you select certain very key variables and measure only those.

4. Ideally it uses items of information that already exist or which you can capture easily as part of some ongoing work process, rather than having to create a whole new system just to measure some activity.

5. The measurement yardsticks you use make sense to the people whose results you are measuring. They can see immediately how getting a good score on a particular functional measure will translate into service quality the customer will appreciate.

These criteria may seem a bit abstract at first until you look at some specific examples of how they work. It helps sometimes to look at the kinds of mistakes managers often make in measuring performance and in setting standards for people.

One of the most common measurement fallacies is the quantity-equals-quality trap. The head of a word processing unit, for example, may believe that the number of pages processed per day or week is a good measure of service quality.

However, pages per day is merely a measure of demand, not of quality. It's an introverted measure rather than an extraverted one. It may satisfy items three and four of the criteria mentioned above, but it doesn't meet the others. To get a clear idea of the fallacy of quantity-equals-quality thinking, just ask this question: "If the number of pages per day goes down on one particular day, does that mean that service quality went down?" The answer is "not necessarily." It might only mean that the volume of business from the customer departments dropped over the previous few days. It may be right after a holiday season or a long weekend, when people are not churning out things to be word processed.

If the manager keeps a chart on the wall showing pages per day over time, the graph may not reflect service quality—as perceived by the customers—at all. There may be a number of other more significant factors, some of which may be highly subjective or qualitative, which dominate the perception of quality.

On the other hand, the manager might choose to measure backlog, or number of days between submission of the work and delivery of the finished product, as a more appropriate variable.

If the customer research showed that response time is very important to the customers, then the average number of days or hours they have to wait might be a more useful quality measure than pages per day.

The manager could go even further and recognize that some customers might be in a big hurry sometimes, and others might not. Perhaps a useful quality measurement would be _delivery time against expectations._ In other words, if we promised the job back to the customer within three working days, did we do as well or better than our promise? At a statistical level, what percentage of our deliveries were equal to or ahead of the promise?

Quality measures like these have a more natural "feel,"

because they immediately imply the kind of action to take if we're not satisfied with our performance on them. In the case of delivery time against expectations, for instance, we may want to look at the process by which we set and communicate the expectation to the customer. Is somebody making unreasonable promises? Is the customer making assumptions which nobody knows about? Is the scheduling process falling down somewhere? Is the staffing level stable?

This type of thinking process, although applied in the above example to a fairly simple "production" type of service, applies in very much the same way to other kinds of service organizations.

In this chapter we'll identify some simple steps to take that can enable you to measure service quality and functional performance in some very natural ways with minimum disruption to the operation.

Again, it is important to shift the point of view from the *activities* of the operation to the *outcomes* of the operation. Ask yourself, "Which measures of our service represent value for our customers?" "How do *they* look at the issue of service quality?" And "How does our output enable them to meet their missions better?"

With this shift in point of view comes a clearer understanding of service quality standards. You need to zero in on those key quality parameters that make the difference. When you have identified them, you can then think in terms of measurable performance standards, both qualitative and quantitative.

Probably the best way to establish some concrete service standards is to start with the critical outcomes at the customer interface and work backward toward the operations in your organization that produce those outcomes. Try to identify one or two key quality parameters that are visible to the customer and set some performance criteria for them. Be sure to key these criteria to the value the outcomes have for the customer.

For example, if speed of response is critical, find out how fast is fast enough. After a certain amount of delay, your results may become useless to your customer. But, on the other hand, doing things faster than a certain standard may not be adding value for the customer. They may not really benefit from ultrafast performance, so you need to think about the costs and impacts of doing it that fast. Are you spending too much in the way of resources, trying to exceed standards that are basically adequate? Whether you set qualitative standards or quantitative standards, be sure to make them as concrete, specific, and observable as possible. Don't go overboard with numerical measurements, but do use them strategically to capture the essence of your particular service quality.

SETTING UP A SERVICE QUALITY MEASUREMENT SYSTEM

Obviously, the service quality measurement approach you develop will arise from the quality standards you have chosen as your navigation guides. Recalling the previous discussion of the "customer report card," we can see the importance of setting down on paper a few key quality attributes you can use in communicating with your staff about performance. In essence, your customer report card is the foundation of your service quality measurement system, or SQMS.

Take each of the quality attributes you identified as part of your customer report card, and decide how you're going to measure it in the simplest, most direct, and economical way. Start by deciding whether you can measure the attribute by direct observation, without having to bother your customers for the feedback. Figure out how to capture the information you need by tapping into some ongoing process in some way. Or you might want to incorporate a quality recording process into the job activities of certain key employees, so you can get the data routinely and automatically.

In cases where the service activity includes processing data with a personal computer, consider adding a quality field into the database or customer record your people are using and have them enter the quality data as part of the basic job. Then you can have quality analyses performed on the data without disturbing the activities of the staff. This approach also has the benefit of conditioning people to be quality minded, because they deal with quality data every time they look at the computer screen.

For some of the service attributes on the report card, you'll somehow have to enlist the aid of your customers to get regular data about the quality of your performance. If your service involves frequent performance of special tasks or projects, consider asking your customers a few basic evaluation questions at the conclusion of every one.

They can be fairly simple questions like, "Overall, how pleased were you with the service we provided?" "Were there any aspects of the service you were especially pleased about, and, if so, what were they and why were you pleased?" "Were there any aspects you were displeased with, and, if so, what were they and why were you not satisfied?" "Could we have done anything better or differently to meet your needs?" You can also ask a few key questions about selected attributes of the service.

One of the easiest ways to get this data is simply to have the staff member who handles the final moment of truth, when the customer "takes delivery" of the service, ask a few questions right on the spot. These should be brief, to the point, and presented in a friendly way. Don't be discouraged if the feedback is rather sparse from many customers. People who are basically satisfied or fairly pleased may not comment in any great detail. But the disgruntled ones and the very pleased ones probably will, and those are the ones you need to learn from.

You might want to set up your service quality measurement system on an informal basis at first, with the results coming to you for study. After a few months of observing certain quality factors, you might want to change your mind about your measurement approach. It's usually better to get measurement systems well worked out first before indoctrinating the staff on their use, for several reasons.

For one, they'll get confused and probably resentful if you keep changing the procedures on them. They'll think you don't really know what you're doing, which will probably be true. It's usually best to have the measurement and feedback process well thought out before you approach them with it.

And second, you'll have a better system if you take some time to work with it. Simplify it, streamline it, and make it easy and comfortable to use. Once you're confident that it provides the kind of service quality picture you and your staff need, then you can implement it with firmness and determination. You'll know it's a system that does the job for everybody with minimum extra effort and minimum distraction from the service mission.

FEEDBACK: HOW TO KEEP ALL EYES ON THE PRIZE

An old one-liner from the psychological theory of transactional analysis goes, "What you stroke is what you get." It means that people in your organization respond to whatever you emphasize on a constant basis and whatever you praise them for. Whatever you're on about is what they'll be on about.

So decide that you're going to be on about accomplishing the department's service mission in an outstanding fashion, and, sooner or later, they'll be on about it too. That is, they'll be on about it if you show them, tell them, and stroke them for it on a constant, never-ending basis.

Feedback tends to work best, in terms of influencing people toward the mission you have established, if you have set up a very clear context for it ahead of time. By conditioning people to think in terms of outstanding service to your organization's customers on a day-to-day basis, you can make them more receptive and more responsive to the feedback. They know it's important, so when you praise them or recognize them for their contributions, they know they're being appreciated for something that's important to the overall success of the organization. You can condition the environment for feedback in a number of ways.

First, you might pick out a simple statement that captures the essence of the commitment you want people in your department to have. Be sure to make it meaningful, nontrivial, and fairly snappy. Don't choose some tired platitude, or it won't work for you. Then start using that statement at every plausible opportunity in discussions with your staff. Tuck it into your conversation. Put it in your memos. Use it whenever you're delivering one of your sermons on service at a staff meeting.

Consider this example, but don't use this expression; find your own. You could say something like, "Everything we do must help our customers do their jobs better. That's the only reason we exist."

Assume that each person in your group will have to hear you say your service "slogan" about 10 times or so before he or she begins to become fairly conscious of it. The next 10 repetitions may begin to lodge it in the minds of most of them. Then the next 10 repetitions may well begin to influence their behavior. By that point, some of them may even begin saying it themselves. Of course, some of them may just throw it back at you whenever they want to make a case for something they're complaining about, but that's at least a start. After you say it long enough and often enough, it will begin to encroach on their conscious as well as unconscious processes.

Next, pick out a simple question and begin asking it repeatedly.

Again, only as an example, how about something like, "What's the best thing we can do for the customer in this instance?" This will focus their attention on the customer rather than on the internal procedures or tasks. It will also put them into an active thinking mode. Whereas the preaching slogan reminds them of the mission, the question slogan forces them to become mentally involved with the mission.

Here are two points of caution on both of the foregoing suggestions. First, don't trivialize the issue by talking to people in platitudes that insult their intelligence. Make what you say meaningful to them. Second, don't underestimate the impact of slogans. The term *slogan* often carries a cynical connotation, but it doesn't have to. Simple, direct, powerful statements that carry the essence of an important idea and which have emotionally appealing overtones can have a very positive effect on people's actions.

The third thing you can do to set up a reinforcing environment for service excellence, if you have subordinate managers, is to recruit them—or "shanghai" them if necessary—into helping you push the service mission. Sit down with them and review the importance of the service idea and let them know that your commitment will continue over the long term, no matter what day-to-day obstacles and distractions come up. Ask them to brainstorm ideas to dramatize the service concept and to think up ways to recognize and appreciate the outstanding performers.

Once you've done some of these things, or even simultaneously with doing them, get the feedback flowing. Make it a policy that you and your managers will devote extra attention to noticing the good things your people do for the customers. If you see something especially noteworthy, be sure to make a comment to that person's supervisor. This will get back to the employee through the supervisor, which has extra value.

Don't be reluctant to praise people on the spot for what they do. The old adage about praising in public and criticizing in private still makes sense. In discussing the work with employees, steer the subject toward customer satisfaction and remind them how you appreciate what they do.

When you talk to your department's customers, actively shop for feedback, especially compliments you can share with the staff. Ask them specifically what they like about the way your people take care of their needs. Be open to critical feedback as well, but transfer that type of information to the staff more carefully, in the context of finding opportunities to improve. If a customer manager praises one of your staff highly, ask him or her to send you a short memo about it. Offer to do the same on behalf of one of his or her staff if it's appropriate. There's nothing quite like documentary evidence to make a point.

If you get such a memo, use it twice. First, show it to the staff member in the presence of his or her boss. Take a few minutes to go over it. Don't just toss it at the person and say, "Good job." Make a miniature ceremony out of it, but don't do it the same way every time. You may be surprised how good the staff worker will feel if you really dwell on the accomplishment for a few minutes, emphasize its importance, and express your appreciation.

The second time you can use a customer memo or expression of appreciation is at a staff meeting. Even though you have mentioned it to the employee and his or her boss, bring it up again. Set aside a few minutes of every staff meeting to talk about service quality. This is a good opportunity to read the memo or note from the customer manager and again congratulate the employee. Little events like these can go a long way toward reinforcing your commitment to quality.

More specifically, share customer evaluation data with the staff on a regular basis. If you've gone the whole way with a service quality measurement system, and you've developed and implemented your customer report card, then you'll have some performance data you can share with them. Make this performance information a regular part of the management data you use in running the department. Share it freely with your managers, and ask them to share it with the people in their groups.

Consider having periodic departmental meetings with all staff as part of your overall approach to departmental affairs. You might do this quarterly, for example. Report to them on what's been happening over the last period, how the department is doing against its goals, and how it stands in the eyes of the customers. This can be a good opportunity to ceremonialize the value of excellent service. Single out the best performers for special recognition and appreciation.

During such a gathering, make a special effort to let everyone in the organization know you appreciate the contributions they're making. Thank them for doing the job well. If you're proud of them, tell them so. It may seem like a small thing, but if you do it with a bit of style, they'll feel good about it.

ROLE MODELS: FIND AND FEED YOUR WATER-WALKERS

Make it clear to everyone in the organization from the outset, by what you say and what you do, that the people who are going to get ahead are the ones who make the best contribution to the mission. They will get the praise, the recognition, the appreciation. They will get the best jobs and projects to work on. They will be the ones you depend on for special missions.

They will have more opportunities to develop their abilities, learn more skills, and advance more quickly.

Do your best to make the difference in performance show up in the pay envelope as well. Over the long run, those who make the best overall contribution to the organization's mission should earn more as well as receive more of the intangible rewards.

How do you find your "water-walkers," the ones who do the service job in an outstanding way? Start with your own perceptions, which are probably fairly accurate. If you're new in your position, you may have to do a bit of guesswork at the start. Make a list of the names of all the people in your organization. Arrange the list in order of the degree of commitment and effectiveness you believe you observe on the part of each of them. Commitment and effectiveness may not be the same thing in some cases, so take that into account. If a person is highly committed, in your view, but not necessarily as effective as he or she might be, keep that person near the top of the list. That commitment will provide a good starting point for development.

Once you have your list, look at the names at the top and the names at the bottom. These are the two best places to start. You can work on the people in the middle in due course. Start with the ones on the bottom. Think carefully about each of them, and ask yourself how well you know their capabilities as well as their commitment. If they work for managers who report to you, discuss their situations with their bosses.

Make up your mind right now that there is no place in your organization for a person who can't or won't contribute to the accomplishment of your service mission. It is your responsibility as a manager to see to it that everyone working for you is working effectively or is on the road to getting there. This is a responsibility you have to the organization of which your department is a part, to the people of your organization who are working effectively, to the people who are not, and to yourself as a professional.

All too often, department managers tolerate mediocre or unsatisfactory performance on the part of some workers, sometimes for a long time, simply because they don't have the stomach for the conflict and confrontation they imagine will be involved in trying to get those people working effectively. Sometimes a manager inherits a burned-out employee or an older one who has "retired" but still draws a paycheck. Perhaps the person has been tolerated for so many years by a series of managers that no one feels right about taking him or her on. They may be crabby, irritable, hostile, and uncommunicative, thereby intimidating others into leaving them alone.

Or they may be "nice." The nice old guy or nice old gal who doesn't bother anybody but at the same time doesn't accomplish a damned thing is only slightly better than the crabby one who doesn't accomplish anything. Both are costing money and giving nothing in return for it. If you have people like this in your organization, it's your job to either get them going or get them out.

If a person has been ineffective and unproductive for a long time, you probably owe them a chance to change their ways. It may well be that one or more managers—possibly including you—have let them down by accepting mediocre performance and not demanding enough from them. If this is the case, it may take a transition period for them to wake up and get back to work. If, after a reasonable period of support, encouragement, and development, the person simply doesn't come around, then you need to accept the fact that he or she should be working somewhere else and help them out of the organization.

The fact that your organization may have bureaucratic procedures that make it difficult to terminate an ineffective person is no excuse not to get going on it. If you fail to take action with a person who is not producing, you're telling everyone else in the organization that you'll accept second best. And you're contradicting the message of excellence you've been trying to get them to accept and act on.

Having taken action with the "sinkers," your next priority is to work with the water-walkers. Pick out the top few people whom you regard as outstanding in their commitment to the mission and their effectiveness at doing their parts. Talk to each of them, one by one, on a personal basis. Let them know you have your eye on them and that you consider them high-potential people.

Challenge each of them to do his or her best, to keep improving, and to help lead the others by example. Share with them your plans and your intentions for developing the organization to an outstanding level of service. Ask them for their ideas on how the department can operate more effectively. Acknowledge their ideas and give them credit for the ones you act upon.

You might find yourself in the happy position of looking at your list and concluding that all of your staff members are well committed to quality service and that they all do a good job. Especially if you have a relatively small unit and if you've been emphasizing the importance of a service orientation right along, you may have no problem people. It may be that all of your people are water-walkers relative to the kinds of performers working in neighboring departments.

In this fortunate circumstance, it may be better to focus on the sense of team spirit and pride that can be a strong motivator and a strong insurance policy for keeping the commitment high. This is the state of affairs you'd like to come to in any case, and you may be fortunate to have the ingredients for it in place at the outset. In this case, there can be a very powerful psychological incentive for paying attention to service quality.

If one person slips a bit, the others will probably convey subtle messages of higher expectations. Give honest praise to the whole group now and then, and tell them how proud of them you are. Even encourage a bit of internal bragging; it's good for team spirit.

But, if you find that you have some developmental work to do with some of the people near the bottom of your original list, as is more likely to be the case, you'll probably find you can make more progress with them by having the water-walkers to point to as role models. This is not to say that you should imply to them that they are somehow inferior and they should feel badly when they compare themselves to the top people. Rather, the message should be that the exemplary members of the team are worth watching and learning from; they have developed the attitudes, skills, and habits of outstanding service and it's worthwhile to study their actions.

There is also a message between the lines, so to speak, that says, "Take a look at the outstanding service performers. Note that they tend to get better treatment when it comes to working conditions, job assignments, opportunities for training and development, praise and recognition, personal privileges, and compensation. If that's what you want for yourself, you can see what you have to do to get it."

RE-EDUCATING, REMINDING, AND REINFORCING

"How soon we forget," the old classic line goes. The unfortunate fact is that outstanding service, especially within organizations, does not come naturally. Left without leadership and emphasis, the level of service in most organizations will regress to a general level of mediocrity.

In the words of the late J. W. Marriott, Sr., "Success is never final." He believed you have to work just as hard to stay at the top as you did to get there.[1] And this applies to the quality of service in your organization.

If you don't want to see the fruits of your efforts disappear over time and watch your organization gradually slip back into bureaucracy and customer hostility, you've got to keep at it. Like it or not, you'll probably see things come to a point where the bloom wears off a bit. The sense of pride, commitment, and specialness is hard to maintain over a long time.

Some people leave, new people come in, and things change. You may get preoccupied or overwhelmed with a big project or a series of business crises that demand your attention. You may begin to take things for granted a bit yourself. It may have been quite some time since you had everyone together and talked about how important it is to do the best possible job. You may have been neglecting to give special praise and recognition to those who deserve it.

You may not have recited your special slogans and given your inspiring lectures for some time. Things are going along basically OK, but the old energy might not still be there. And one day, you'll overhear one of your staff on the telephone dealing with a customer in an uncooperative way. He or she may be refusing to do something out of the ordinary or may be insisting that the customer follow some departmental procedure or trying to brush the customer off and get out of doing something special or unusual.

Then you'll get a funny feeling that you may have fallen asleep at the switch. You may feel a bit disappointed in the staff member or in others in the organization. You may think, "I thought we were all committed to the cause. I've said it loud enough and long enough. I thought we'd achieved an outstanding level of service." But you're witnessing the erosion of the commitment. The dream is starting to fade. The drama, the magic, the enthusiasm—they're all starting to fade a bit. It's time for a second wind. It's time for renewal.

And you have to begin doing some of the same things all over again. Review the commitment and performance of everyone, especially the newcomers. Have you really gotten them on the team? Have the systems and procedures taken over? Have they become customer hostile instead of customer friendly? Have you given them the attention they deserve? Have you been emphasizing the mission and the commitment to excellence as often as you should?

In a way, service excellence is just like physical fitness. You have to keep at it. Just as you start to get out of shape as soon as you stop exercising, so too do you start to lose the quality of service as soon as you stop emphasizing it, praising it, and feeding and watering it. You have to educate, re-educate, remind, and reinforce on a regular basis. The newcomers and the old timers both need to hear it from you—forever. As soon as you stop talking about it, they're likely to drift into the assumption that it's no longer as important to you. Make sure they know how you feel about it, all the time.

CHAPTER NOTES

1. For an enlightening interview with J. W. "Bill" Marriott, Jr., who quotes extensively from his famous father's business philosophy, see Karl Albrecht, *At America's Service: How Corporations Can Revolutionize the Way They Treat Their Customers* (Homewood, Ill.: Dow Jones–Irwin, 1988), p. 225.

INDEX